Insight S
Catric

Animal Farm

George Orwell

insight

insight

George Orwell's Animal Farm by Catriona Mills
Insight Study Guide series

Copyright © 2011 Insight Publications Pty Ltd

First published in 2011 by
Insight Publications Pty Ltd
ABN 57 005 102 983
89 Wellington Street
St Kilda VIC 3182
Australia
Tel: +61 3 9523 0044
Fax: +61 3 9523 2044
Email: books@insightpublications.com
Website: www.insightpublications.com

This edition published 2011 in the United States of America by
Insight Publications Pty Ltd, Australia.

ISBN-13: 978-1-921411-81-6

Library of Congress Control Number: 2011931337

Cover Design by The Modern Art Production Group
Cover Illustrations by The Modern Art Production Group,
istockphoto® and House Industries
Internal Design by Sarn Potter

Printed in the United States of America by Lightning Source
10 9 8 7 6 5 4 3 2 1

contents

Character map iv

Overview 1

    About the author 1

    Synopsis 3

    Character summaries 4

Background & context 6

Genre, structure & language 11

Chapter-by-chapter analysis 15

Characters & relationships 32

Themes, ideas & values 42

Different interpretations 53

Questions & answers 58

Sample answer 65

References & reading 68

CHARACTER MAP

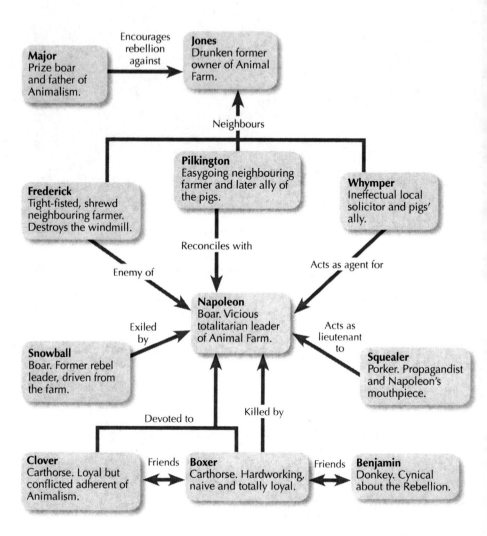

OVERVIEW

About the author

'George Orwell' was the pen name of Eric Arthur Blair. He was born in 1903 in India (then a British colony). His parents were Richard Walmesley Blair (who worked in the Opium Department of the Indian Civil Service) and Ida Mabel Limouzin. While Richard completed his term of service in India, Ida and her children returned to England, where Orwell later attended Eton, one of England's oldest and most famous public schools.

In 1921, he left Eton and joined the Indian Imperial Police in Burma, an experience that inspired *Burmese Days* (1934), a novel that explored the corruption and tyranny of British imperialism. After returning to England, he spent some time moving among the poorer inhabitants of Paris and London, which formed the basis of his first published book, *Down and Out in Paris and London* (1933). As the book is written from the perspective of an unidentified narrator, Blair required a pseudonym: he chose 'George Orwell', the name under which all his future works would be published.

Orwell was hospitalised twice with pneumonia between 1927 and 1933, a forerunner of the lung problems that would lead to his early death. Convinced to give up teaching, with which he had been supplementing his income, Orwell recuperated at his mother's house in Southwold, Suffolk. It was here that he wrote the experimental novel *The Clergyman's Daughter* (1935), with which he was deeply unsatisfied.

After finishing this novel, Orwell returned to London, where he worked part-time at a bookshop in Hampstead. This experience provided some of the background for *Keep the Aspidistra Flying* (1936), a novel whose neurotic protagonist unsuccessfully pursues a bohemian lifestyle after developing a distaste for the trappings of respectability.

In London Orwell met his wife, Eileen O'Shaughnessy, a former teacher with a psychology degree from Oxford University and a background in social work working with London prostitutes. During this time Orwell's engagement with politics strengthened: he remained devoted to democratic socialism for the rest of his life. In 1936 he travelled to the north of England, an area suffering badly during the Great Depression. The result of his observations was *The Road to Wigan Pier* (1937), a book that was partly a sociological survey of living and working conditions in the north and partly an analysis of socialism's role in improving these conditions.

Orwell left England in December 1936 to observe the Spanish Civil War (1936–39), in which conservative generals (led by Francisco Franco) rebelled against the government of President Manuel Azaña. Though the British government refused to intervene directly in the conflict, the war attracted socialist sympathisers from across Europe, including several thousand volunteers from Great Britain and Ireland.

Orwell did not long remain an observer; he joined first the POUM (Workers' Party of Marxist Unification) and then the International Brigades (made up of non-Spanish volunteers). During his time with the POUM, Orwell witnessed squabbling among various branches of the Communist Party, including widespread arrests of Leon Trotsky's supporters. The self-destructiveness of this behaviour, when they were facing a common enemy in the Fascist rebels, influenced *Animal Farm* and *Nineteen Eighty-Four*, the works for which he is best remembered. While fighting on the Aragon Front in 1937, Orwell was shot in the throat by a sniper. Badly wounded, he recuperated briefly before returning to England in June 1937. His experiences in Spain were published as *Homage to Catalonia* (1938).

In 1938 Orwell was diagnosed with tuberculosis. For his health, he and his wife began to spend more time in warmer countries while Orwell continued to write and publish, including the novel *Coming Up For Air* (1939) and numerous essays.

When World War II broke out, Orwell's lung condition made him unfit for military service. Instead, he worked as a programmer at the BBC, counteracting German propaganda. While there, he began writing *Animal Farm*. When it was eventually published in August 1945, its success made Orwell a sought-after figure in both Great Britain and the United States.

In March 1945 Eileen died under anaesthetic during a hysterectomy. Orwell and his adopted son Richard moved to the isle of Jura (part of the Inner Hebrides, an archipelago off the west coast of Scotland) in 1946.

Here, Orwell wrote the novel *Nineteen Eighty-Four* (1949), a dystopian tale of government surveillance, mind control and perpetual war.

Orwell's health deteriorated steadily; from 1947 onwards he was frequently hospitalised. In January 1949 he entered a sanatorium in Gloucestershire, but was removed in September to University College Hospital, where he married his second wife, Sonia Brownell. Orwell planned to travel to Switzerland, where sanatoriums treated tuberculosis patients at high altitude, but, on 21 January 1950, an artery burst in his lungs, killing him at age 46.

Synopsis

Major, the prize boar at Mr Jones's Manor Farm, collects the other farm animals together and tells them of his previous night's dream. He tells them that revolution is coming, in which the tyranny of Man will be overthrown. Soon after Major's death, the pigs – particularly the boars Snowball and Napoleon – develop a political system that they term Animalism. Though the animals are not actively planning a revolution, they overthrow Mr Jones one night when he returns home drunk and neglects to feed them.

The animals rename the farm 'Animal Farm' and inscribe the Seven Commandments of Animalism on the barn wall. Even in the earliest stages of the Rebellion, the pigs claim particular privileges for themselves. For the first summer, the animals are happy and the new system is successful. News of the revolution spreads to neighbouring farms, where animals are severely punished for singing revolutionary songs. Mr Jones attempts to reclaim his farm, but is defeated by the animals in the Battle of the Cowshed.

Dissension among the pigs, centred around Snowball's plans to build a windmill to reduce the animals' workload, culminates in Snowball being run off the farm by Napoleon's secret police (the dogs). After Snowball's expulsion, Napoleon abandons democratic meetings. The animals work harder than ever, but they cannot keep up with the harvest while also building the windmill. The pigs begin to modify the commandments of Animalism for their own advantage.

The windmill collapses and Napoleon holds show trials in which various animals confess to working against him and are executed. The terrified animals work at rebuilding the windmill but, when Napoleon enters into trade with neighbouring farmers, one of them cheats him of his lumber and then blows up the windmill.

The animals again work to rebuild the windmill, though Boxer the carthorse is injured and their rations are severely reduced. As the work grows harder, Boxer becomes increasingly unwell. He looks forward to his retirement, but when he collapses hauling stone, Napoleon has him sent away for slaughter.

Years pass and many of the animals die, until few are left who actually remember the revolution. The pigs begin to walk on their hind legs, and the other animals notice that all the commandments of Animalism are gone, replaced by the legend ALL ANIMALS ARE EQUAL, BUT SOME ANIMALS ARE MORE EQUAL THAN OTHERS. The pigs adopt clothing, and Napoleon invites the neighbouring farmers to tour the farm. As the humans and pigs drink and play cards together in the evening, the watching animals realise they can no longer tell the difference between the men and the pigs.

Character summaries

Napoleon: Berkshire boar; one of the leaders of the Rebellion and, after Snowball's expulsion, sole leader. Totalitarian and vicious, he is protected by a pack of trained dogs and supported by Squealer's propaganda (see **Themes, Ideas & Values**).

Snowball: Boar; one of the early leaders of the Rebellion, later expelled by Napoleon. Though committed to the principles of Animalism, he is not above accepting small luxuries. After his expulsion, he becomes a terrifying bogeyman to the remaining animals.

Squealer: Porker who works as the pigs' propagandist, convincing the other animals that the pigs are working for all the animals' benefit. A nimble, shrill-voiced pig, he is a brilliant and persuasive speaker.

Boxer: Carthorse; enormously strong and of steady character, but not particularly intelligent. He remains devoted to the principles of the Rebellion until the moment when he is driven to the knacker's yard.

Benjamin: Donkey; the oldest and one of the cleverest animals on the farm. Bad tempered and devoted to Boxer, he is cynical about the Rebellion from the start.

Clover: Carthorse; approaching middle age at the beginning of the novella. Devoted to the principles of Animalism, yet she is increasingly uncertain about their application.

Mr Jones: Farmer, whose increasing drunkenness and neglect of his animals prompts the Rebellion. He tries but fails to regain Manor Farm, and dies in a home for alcoholics.

Mr Whymper: Solicitor from the neighbouring town of Willingdon. A sly man and largely unsuccessful solicitor, he is cunning enough to exploit the animals' need for a human agent.

Mr Pilkington: A 'gentleman farmer' who owns the neglected farm of Foxwood, bordering Animal Farm. Primarily interested in hunting and fishing, he is reconciled with Napoleon at the end of the novella.

Mr Frederick: The owner of Pinchfield Farm, bordering Animal Farm. A shrewd man with a reputation for driving hard bargains and having a fondness for lawsuits, he cheats Napoleon in a lumber deal and destroys the second windmill.

Major: Middle White boar, show pig and breeding pig. He introduces the animals to the principles of Animalism after a prophetic dream. Dies early in the novella, but remains significant to the animals until late in Napoleon's rule.

BACKGROUND & CONTEXT

The Russian Revolution

Though *Animal Farm* draws inspiration from multiple totalitarian regimes – both fascist (right wing) and communist (left wing) – the Russian Revolution of 1917, which created Soviet Russia, is a particularly strong influence. The following is a brief overview of the revolution, particularly the causes and events that are echoed in Orwell's novella.

'Russian Revolution' is the collective name for several revolutions in 1917, most significantly the February Revolution (which took place in March according to the Gregorian calendar; at the time Russia was using the Julian calendar) and the October Revolution (in November). The revolutions brought about the end of tsarist rule in Russia. Russian tsars were absolute monarchs: they held all state power, although people and institutions acted in their name (since it was impossible for the tsar to make all decisions personally). Tsars were the supreme authority on religious matters (where most other European leaders were subject to the Pope) and owned a high proportion of state lands and industry.

The causes of the Russian Revolution are complicated, but Russian dissatisfaction with the tsars first turned to violence in the Russian Revolution of 1905, a period of socio-political upheaval marked by massive strikes and military mutinies. The 1905 revolution changed the nature of tsarist authority: Tsar Nicholas II agreed to form the State Duma (parliament) of the Russian Empire, making Russia a constitutional monarchy. However, the Duma was a consultative body with limited power and, as some protests during the revolution had been oppressed brutally – notably on Bloody Sunday, when hundreds of peaceful protestors outside the Winter Palace were killed by troops – people remained dissatisfied.

Dissatisfaction increased during World War I (1914–18), when financial crises led to rapid inflation and lack of food, and was exacerbated when Tsar Nicholas II focused on his position as commander-in-chief, leaving his wife, the Empress, in charge of daily government. Empress Alexandra Feodorovna (née Alix of Hesse) was an unpopular ruler: she was German at a time when Russia was at war with Germany; she was a strong believer in autocracy, equally reluctant to either relinquish any of her authority or court the people's approval; and she was strongly associated with the monk Grigori Rasputin.

The details of Rasputin's life and his influence on the Empress are difficult to establish with any certainty, because so much is based on hearsay or has become mythologised. (For example, in 1916, Rasputin's assassins are widely believed to have poisoned, beaten and repeatedly shot him, before finally drowning him, which gives him a mythic, demonic status. In all likelihood, he was beaten before being fatally shot.) However, he was certainly hated and feared by both the Russian elite and the revolutionaries because of the influence he held over the Empress, who believed he could cure her son, the Tsarevitch Alexei Nikolaevich, of his haemophilia (an extremely painful and debilitating blood disorder that, prior to the 1960s, reduced life expectancy to an average of eleven years).

These circumstances (and others) led to the revolutions of 1917. The first – the February Revolution – began as strikes and demonstrations in Petrograd (St Petersburg). Tsar Nicholas II ordered the military (traditionally loyal directly to him) to suppress the rioters by force. He had also recently stripped the Duma of legislative authority; these acts marked a return to pre-1905 levels of autocracy. Troops mutinied, refusing to open fire on crowds containing many women and children. As the Duma continued to act despite the tsar's orders and more troops joined the mutiny, the tsar was advised by his army chiefs and ministers to abdicate: he did so, first personally and then on behalf of his son, the tsarevitch. The royal family was placed under house arrest and a provisional government was established under the leadership of Prince Georgy Yevgenyevich Lvov, whose appointment was Nicholas II's last official act.

The February Revolution did not stabilise conditions in Russia for long. The socialists had formed a party, the Petrograd Soviet, to rival the Provisional Government. ('Soviet' originally meant 'governmental council', but after the revolution it came to mean 'local council elected by workers'.) Throughout 1917, the Petrograd Soviet came more and more under the influence of the Bolsheviks, a faction of the Marxist Russian Social Democratic Party. The Bolsheviks were founded in 1905 by Vladimir Ilyich Lenin, though they had played only a small role in the 1905 revolution.

Popular support for the Petrograd Soviet increased as it came under the control of the Bolsheviks, since the Bolsheviks were the sole major party not to compromise with the weakening Provisional Government. In October (September by the Russian calendar), the Bolsheviks called for the dissolution of the Provisional Government, and in November (October by the Russian calendar), Lenin led his supporters in a successful revolt, marking the beginning of Soviet rule in Russia, now under the control of Lenin.

The October Revolution did not lead to undisputed Soviet control of Russia; rather, it initiated the Russian Civil War (1917–23) in which the Bolshevik Red Army battled the liberal, monarchist White Army. (The White Army had little chance, however, of restoring the monarchy, since Nicholas II, his wife, his four daughters, and his son were all executed by firing squad in July 1918.) In 1924, shortly after the end of the Civil War, Lenin (who had survived two assassination attempts) died, to be succeeded by Joseph Stalin, a long-standing member of the Bolshevik party.

Stalin's rivalry with Lenin's former second-in-command, Leon Trotsky, was evident as early as 1918. After Lenin's death, Stalin pushed towards absolute power, beginning by expanding the secret police and overturning Lenin's economic policies in favour of his own. His push for control culminated in the exile of Trotsky (in 1929) and the Great Purge (1936–38), in which hundreds of thousands of parliamentarians and military officers were stripped of power, sentenced in show trials (trials in which the outcome is pre-determined), and executed or exiled. When World War II began in 1939, Stalin wielded political power as absolute as Nicholas II's authority twenty-two years earlier, just as Napoleon, at the end of *Animal Farm*, replaces Jones.

Publishing history

By the time Orwell came to write *Animal Farm*, Stalin was firmly in control in Russia, and Europe was at war. This was the era of totalitarianism, in which powerful European countries were under the control of dictators: Adolf Hitler, *Führer und Reichkanzler* (Leader and Chancellor) of

Germany from 1934 until his suicide in 1945; Benito Mussolini, *Il Duce* (The Leader) of Italy between 1925 and his deposition in 1943; Francisco Franco, *Caudillo de España* (Leader of Spain) between 1936 and 1975; and Joseph Stalin, General Secretary of the Communist Party of the Soviet Union between 1922 and 1953. Of these, only Mussolini was no longer in power when Orwell wrote *Animal Farm*, and he was executed in 1945. *Animal Farm* draws strongly from Russian history and circumstances, but is also flavoured by these other totalitarian regimes. (For more details of how Orwell draws from various totalitarian regimes, see the **Chapter-by-Chapter Analysis**.)

Because *Animal Farm* was written and published during World War II, it had a fraught publishing history. Orwell wrote the novella between November 1943 and February 1944, in the heart of World War II. By inscribing these dates before the words 'The End', Orwell makes them part of the novella itself, marking it as belonging to a highly specific time and place. During the four months in which Orwell was writing, the outcome of World War II was still very much undecided. France (whose border with Germany made it vulnerable to the invading German armies) had formally surrendered in June 1940, but the United States had entered the war after the Japanese attack on Pearl Harbor in December 1941, and the situation was still uncertain. Furthermore, both sides of the conflict included totalitarian states, a form of power with which Orwell was distinctly uncomfortable. This discomfort became dominant in *Animal Farm* – 'the first book,' wrote Orwell, 'in which I tried, with full consciousness of what I was doing, to fuse political purpose and artistic purpose into one whole' (Orwell, 2004, p.10).

Numerous publishers in both the United Kingdom and the United States rejected *Animal Farm*. Some rejected it on the grounds that there was no market for children's books: before fantasy fiction emerged as a discrete genre during the 1950s, many authors whose works contained fantasy elements were classified as children's writers (for example, JRR Tolkien, with *The Lord of the Rings*). Others rejected the work because they feared offending the Russian government at a time when Russia was a crucial ally in the war against Germany and the Axis powers. The novella was not published until 17 August 1945 in the United Kingdom (after both Germany and Japan had surrendered) and a year later in the United States.

By the time *Animal Farm* was published in the United States, the Cold War had begun: a period of tension and indirect conflict, lasting until 1991, between NATO countries (dominated by the United States) and Eastern bloc countries (dominated by Russia), which led to strong anti-communist feelings, particularly in the United States. *Animal Farm* was written at a time in which totalitarian states were locked in conflict, imbuing it with a strong anti-totalitarian rhetoric. But the longevity of Stalin's rule (compared to the fascist dictatorships of Hitler and Mussolini) and of the Cold War that followed World War II have perhaps influenced tendencies to read *Animal Farm* as exclusively a critique of Russian communism.

GENRE, STRUCTURE & LANGUAGE

Genre

Animal Farm is often called a 'beast fable' (see **Vocabulary**), but Orwell himself chose to give his novella the prominent subtitle 'a fairy story'. In the American first edition and most translations published in Orwell's lifetime, the subtitle was dropped or altered. But *Animal Farm* makes rich use of fairytale conventions and the various ways in which the term 'fairytale' has come to be applied.

Like beast fables, fairytales were once general literature, but have come to be associated with children. Orwell's difficulties in getting the novella published (see **Background & Context**) show the twentieth-century assumption that fairytales are for children. 'Fairytale' is a fairly modern term for an old form of narrative, a type of folktale. Not all fairytales involve fairies, which is why some critics prefer the German term *Märchen* ('wonder tale').

Fairytales (like other forms of folktale) were originally oral, rather than written texts. In this sense, the 'fairytale' in *Animal Farm* is not only the novella itself, but also the way in which narratives work in the novella. Apart from the pigs and dogs, only Muriel the goat and Benjamin the donkey learn to read with any skill, and neither can use writing implements. The pigs' advanced literacy therefore gives them control over the written history of the Rebellion: the official history of Animal Farm exists in Squealer's lists, Minimus' poems and the (gradually amended) commandments. In a sense, this official history is also a 'fairytale', in the colloquial use of the term to mean an incredible or misleading statement.

But there's a second narrative buried within *Animal Farm*, one that, like traditional fairytales, exists in oral form. Because the other animals struggle with reading and writing, they tell the story over and over, to themselves and to their new comrades:

> When they heard the gun booming and saw the green flag fluttering at the masthead, their hearts swelled with imperishable pride, and the talk turned always towards the old heroic days,

the expulsion of Jones, the writing of the Seven Commandments, the great battles in which the human invaders had been defeated (pp.87–88).

These oral histories keep a second narrative alive on the farm: the story of the Rebellion, the hoped-for utopia of animals that will now never come about, because the pigs have moved so far from the early principles of Animalism. These oral histories, too, are fairytales: tales of wonders that never came to pass.

The animals' stories of the Rebellion and the secret singing of 'Beasts of England' are also subversive, since they are counter to the formal history that Napoleon endorses. But, as folklorist Jack Zipes points out, traditional fairytales are subversive:

> ... the focus is on class struggle and competition for power among the aristocrats themselves and the peasantry and the aristocracy ... *He* who has power can exercise *his* will, right wrongs, become ennobled, amass money and land, win women as prizes and social prestige (Zipes, 1991, p.8).

Zipes' argument, simply, is that in fairytales the clever peasant can become a king. In *Animal Farm*, a clever pig destined for slaughter can become a landowner. Such endings have led to the term 'fairytale' becoming synonymous with 'happy ending' (as in 'a fairytale wedding'). But in this case, as in so much of his writing, Orwell's use of the term is ironic: this fairytale has no happy ending, not even for the pigs, who end by quarrelling viciously with their new allies.

Structure

Fairytales usually have a linear narrative: the clever peasant from the story's beginning is, by the end, a king. *Animal Farm*'s narrative is both linear and cyclical. Some aspects of the novella show linear progression: Boxer grows old, weakens, and dies; the pigs' power increases; the farm expands and becomes rich. But the narrative is ultimately cyclical: the end brings us back to the beginning. Not even the fact that the new landlords are pigs is an advance from the farm's condition at the beginning of the novella, because by its end, the men and pigs are interchangeable.

This cyclical structure reinforces the melancholic tone of the novella. During their tribulations, the animals have comforted themselves with the fact that they are their own masters. They cling to the idea of progress, of some significant change between their former wretched state and their current wretched state. In the final chapter, they take pride in the fact that, 'They were still the only farm in the whole country – in all England! – owned and operated by animals' (p.87). But the narrative's cyclical structure undercuts even this comfort. As the animals watch the meeting between men and pigs, Napoleon explains the situation to the men: 'This farm which he had the honour to control, he added, was a co-operative enterprise. The title-deeds, which were in his own possession, were owned by the pigs jointly' (p.93). The ending of the book signals an absolute return to the beginning.

The novella's cyclical nature is encapsulated in the motif of the windmill, the object on which Snowball centres all his hopes of 'Animal Farm as it might be when sordid labour was lifted from the animals' backs' (p.35). But as the windmill is built, destroyed, rebuilt and destroyed again, it shows that their progress is illusionary: it is simply re-treading the same ground.

Narrative point of view

Animal Farm has a third-person narrative: an anonymous narrator speaks from outside the events. Third-person narrators are defined in terms of two characteristics: objectivity and omniscience. Objectivity is the degree to which the narrator is aware of the characters' inner thoughts. An objective narrator is aware of what a character is doing, but cannot tell what they are thinking; a subjective narrator is aware of the thoughts of one or several of the characters. Omniscience refers to the knowledge possessed by the narrator. A truly omniscient narrator has full knowledge of people and events; a limited narrator is confined to knowledge of one or several characters. Orwell uses a subjective, limited narrator for *Animal Farm* and manipulates the narrator's limits to reinforce his critique of totalitarianism.

For example, he restricts the reader's access to characters' thoughts. Indeed, the only time that we are deeply immersed in a character's head is when Clover sits near the half-finished windmill after the show trials. The subjective narrative stance here involves the reader in the animals' despair at the turning point in the Rebellion in a way that narrating their actions would not do. We are simultaneously aware of Clover's deep loyalty to the principles of Animalism and the way this loyalty traps her in a reality that is far removed from the animals' original plans. But this character, whose thoughts we can see, is a relatively powerless figure. The narrator never shares the thoughts of the pigs with us: they are equally enigmatic to us and to the other animals.

Similarly, using a limited rather than an omniscient narrator reinforces the idea that the farm is a place of secrets, lies, propaganda and rumours. For example, the reader knows that Jones is complaining about the Rebellion (p.24) and that neighbouring farmers are frightened of the Rebellion spreading (p.25). But the animals also know this: this is not an omniscient narrator at work, but an illusion of omniscience brought about by the pigs' spy network (the pigeons). The narrator's refusal or inability to share omniscient knowledge means that the reader is frightened, shocked, or distressed at the same time as the animals. For example, we are unaware of Boxer's fate until we read the sign on the knacker's van, at the same time that Benjamin reads it to the animals (p.82).

To take a more complicated example, consider Napoleon's show trials, when he purges the farm of his enemies. The reader never sees or hears anything about how the victims' confessions have been extorted from them. We assume the confessions have been extorted (through torture or some such means), because we know such practices occurred during the Great Purge in Soviet Russia. But, like the observers at the original trials, all we (and the watching animals) see is a series of apparently spontaneous confessions. Everything else happens behind closed doors, away from the eyes of the limited narrator. The reader is more fortunate than the animals – being outside the novella, knowing that it is an allegory (see **Vocabulary**), we can bring additional knowledge to bear on the novella's events. But during the reading process itself, the focus of the subjective, limited narrator brings us inside the claustrophobia of the police state, where all we know is what a totalitarian leader allows us to know.

CHAPTER-BY-CHAPTER ANALYSIS

Chapter I (pp.1–8)

Summary: *Major the boar prepares the animals for a future uprising against Man and teaches them the revolutionary song, 'Beasts of England'.*

Major is presented as a philosopher, saying to the animals, 'I have had a long life, I have had much time for thought as I lay alone in my stall, and I think I may say that I understand the nature of life on this earth as well as any animal now living' (p.3).

Animal Farm originated in Orwell's idea of analysing Marx's political theories from an animal perspective. Introducing a 1947 edition (titled *Kolghosp Tvaryn*) intended for displaced Ukrainian citizens, he wrote:

> To them [animals] it was clear that the concept of a class struggle between humans was pure illusion, since whenever it was necessary to exploit animals, all humans united against them: the true struggle is between animals and humans.

This summary is the core of old Major's long speech (pp.3–7), where he states, 'all the evils of this life of ours spring from the tyranny of human beings' (p.5).

Major's speech suggests the influence of the Fabian school of socialism.

- The Fabian Society is a British socialist movement (active from the late-nineteenth century and strongly influential in the foundation of the British Labour Party), favouring gradual social change through reform, not violent revolution.

- Fabian socialism drew criticism from other socialists, perhaps most notably Leon Trotsky, who denounced the philosophy in his essay, 'The Fabian "Theory" of Socialism'.

- The Fabian influence is explored in the fact that Major doesn't seek immediate, violent rebellion: 'I do not know when that Rebellion will come, it might be in a week or in a hundred years' (p.5). His main aim is for the animals to be prepared, educated and conscious of their oppressed state: 'pass on this message of mine to those who come after you, so that future generations shall carry on the struggle until it is victorious' (p.5).

Key points

'Comrade' means friend, colleague, or ally. Socialists wanted an egalitarian term to replace forms of address such as 'Mister,' 'Miss,' or 'Mrs', and were inspired by the French Revolution (1789–99), when 'lord' and 'lady' were replaced by 'citizen' (*citoyen* for men and *citoyenne* for women). Socialists adopted the term 'comrade' during the mid-nineteenth century. In the years immediately after the Russian Revolution of 1917, the term 'comrade' was applied specifically to people sympathetic to the revolution (such as members of either the Communist Party or the working classes), and 'citizen' was used as a neutral term for all others. By the mid-1920s, however, this distinction disappeared, and 'comrade' was used indiscriminately.

Key vocabulary

'Clementine': Refers to 'Oh My Darling, Clementine,' an American folk ballad, usually attributed to Percy Montrose and written circa 1884, though based on an earlier song.

Hands: Unit of measurement for horses, equal to four inches or 101.6 millimetres.

'La Cucaracha': Also 'La Cucaracha', a traditional Spanish folk *corrido* (ballad), popular during the Mexican Revolution (1910–20). The lyrics are satirical, and were often improvised to include critiques of contemporary socio-political issues.

Pop-holes: Small doors allowing hens to enter and to leave a henhouse.

Mangel-wurzel: A variety of beet cultivated as livestock food, especially for cattle.

Scullery: Small room or section of a larger pantry, for food preparation and utensil storage.

Trap: British term for a carriage, especially a light, two-wheeled vehicle.

Tushes: The milk tusks (or precursor tusks) of a tusked animal, such as a boar. Orwell presumably means 'tusks,' since Major is too old to still have his milk tusks.

Windsor chair: Chair with a solid wooden seat, into which the back, arms and legs are inserted.

Q How does the behaviour of the animals in this chapter foreshadow their behaviour for the rest of the novella?

Chapter II (pp.9–16)

Summary: *Major dies; the pigs develop his ideas into Animalism; when Jones forgets to feed the animals, they rebel.*

Immediately after Major's death, the animals adhere to his revolutionary ideals:

> They did not know when the Rebellion predicted by Major would take place, they had no reason for thinking that it would be within their own lifetime, but they saw clearly that it was their duty to prepare for it (p.9).

The Rebellion is a spontaneous reaction to the more than usually lax treatment from the drunken Jones.

After the Rebellion, the animals file reverently through the farmhouse, 'afraid to speak above a whisper and gazing with a kind of awe at the unbelievable luxury' (p.14). But a closer look at the furnishings shows the opposite of luxury. The furniture falls into two distinct categories: old or inexpensive.

- Much of the farmhouse furniture is old-fashioned. For example, horsehair sofas were popular during the nineteenth century. Similarly, feather mattresses are from an earlier time: the box spring was invented in the nineteenth century and inner-spring mattresses in the 1930s, both of which made mattresses more comfortable. The Joneses' furnishings seem either old or a thrifty reuse of material readily available on the farm.

- Other items, such as the Brussels carpet and lithograph, are mass produced and therefore less expensive and less luxurious than handmade goods.

These specific items suggest that what the animals consider as luxury is comparatively cheap on a human scale.

Other specific items hint at Jones's political leanings:

- On the evening of the Rebellion, Jones has fallen asleep with the *News of the World* over his face (p.11). The *News of the World* (founded 1843) was a tabloid newspaper, aimed largely at the working classes; by 1939 it had a circulation of four million. Focusing on titillation and shock value rather than hard news stories, it had a distinctly right-wing political agenda.

- The lithograph of Queen Victoria also suggests that Jones is conservative by nature, not only because Victoria's prime ministers were largely conservative, but also because he is looking back to the past, presumably (since the portrait is hung in a dominant position, over the mantelpiece) considering it superior to the modern day.

Jones's conservatism is in opposition to the radical politics of the animals, at least in the early stages of the Rebellion.

Key points

Napoleon takes his name from Napoleon Bonaparte, French military leader and later Emperor of France, whose coup d'état in 1799 plunged much of Europe into the Napoleonic Wars (1803–15). He gave his name to 'Bonapartism,' a political movement advocating a centralised government based on popular support for a strong leader. The word has become an insult in Marxist terminology. Karl Marx used 'Bonapartism' to describe a situation in which military counter-revolutionaries seize power from revolutionaries and then exploit the radical feelings of the working classes to keep themselves in power. (Trotsky, for example, described Stalin's regime as Bonapartist.) The pig's name, Napoleon, therefore, hints at his future behaviour and the outcome of the Rebellion.

Key vocabulary

Blinkers: Part of a horse's harness, designed to restrict its side and rear vision, forcing it to focus on what's in front of it.

Brussels carpet: Machine-made floor covering, particularly fashionable in the nineteenth century.

Horsehair sofa: Sofa stuffed with the coarse hair from the manes and tails of horses.

Lithograph: Picture printed from a metal or stone ink-receptive surface, allowing it to be mass-produced.

Nose rings: Rings inserted between the nostrils of farm animals, either to lead and control dangerous animals (especially bulls) or to prevent destructive animals (especially pigs) digging in the ground with their snouts, destroying turf and crops.

Porker: Sometimes used as a general term for any pig, 'porker' refers to a pig being specifically fattened for food. Orwell clearly indicates that the porkers have been castrated (to increase weight and reduce 'boar taint,' an unpleasant taste to the meat caused by certain chemicals in the fat of a sexually mature boar). 'Porker' is not the most common name for a castrated pig, but Orwell specifies that (after Snowball's expulsion) only Napoleon is able to impregnate sows (p.75).

Spinney: A small wood.

Q Orwell gives his animals both human and animal qualities. Why?

Chapter III (pp.17–23)

Summary: The animals bring in the harvest; Snowball and Napoleon disagree on farm management; the pigs take certain luxuries for themselves.

The first post-Rebellion harvest shows the animals operating as a workers' collective, in which 'every animal down to the humblest worked at turning the hay and gathering it' (p.17).

The Rebellion has a briefly idyllic outcome, with 'the biggest harvest that the farm had ever seen', of which 'not an animal of the farm had stolen so much as a mouthful' (p.17). 'All through that summer the work of the farm went like clockwork' (pp.17–18), because the animals are content with working for themselves, not slaving for Jones.

Orwell simultaneously reinforces the idea of socialism at its idyllic best and shows that idyll being eroded, even this soon after the Rebellion.

- He says of the animals that 'everyone worked according to his capacity' (p.18). This echoes the socialist principle most famously quoted by Karl Marx in 'Critique of the Gotha Program' (1875): 'From each according to his ability, to each according to his needs.'

- But the idea of 'ability' and 'needs' is already being manipulated through Squealer's propaganda. The pigs claim special privileges, namely milk and apples. Squealer translates these privileges into needs: 'We pigs are brainworkers. The whole management and organisation of the farm depend on us. Day and night we are watching over your welfare. It is for *your* sake that we drink that milk and eat those apples' (p.23).
Even this soon after the Rebellion, the pigs disagree:

- Snowball wishes to form the animals into productivity committees and to improve their literacy (pp.20–22). The committees are largely a failure and the literacy programs have mixed results, but these activities show him genuinely working to improve farm conditions.

- Napoleon, conversely, is only interested in 'the education of the young' (p.22), namely the training of the new puppies, the results of which become apparent in Chapter V.

Q To what extent are Napoleon's ambitions evident at this early stage of the novella?

Chapter IV (pp.24–29)

Summary: *Rumours of Animal Farm spread to neighbouring farms; Jones's attempt to return to the farm ends with the Battle of the Cowshed.*

Neighbouring farmers become anxious about the Rebellion and start to spread rumours that, firstly, the animals 'were perpetually fighting among themselves and were also rapidly starving to death' and, secondly, that the animals 'practised cannibalism, tortured one another with red-hot horseshoes and had their females in common' (p.25). One reason for their anxiety might be that neither neighbour is an efficient farmer (see **Characters & Relationships**). Both therefore have a vested interest in maintaining Man's dominance over animals:

- They react badly to the propaganda coming from Animal Farm, from which the pigs 'sent out flights of pigeons, whose instructions were to mingle with the animals on neighbouring farms, tell them the story of the Rebellion, and teach them the tune of "Beasts of England"' (p.24).

- They react particularly strongly to the anthem of the Rebellion: 'The human beings could not contain their rage when they heard this song, though they pretended to think it merely ridiculous' (p.25).

- The intriguing aspect of this is that the humans are aware that their animals comprehend and speak English, are intelligent and can communicate, but continue to treat them as dumb beasts (in this case, flogging any animal heard singing the song).

Some allegorical readings suggest that the Battle of the Cowshed represents the Russian Civil War (see **Background & Context**). Certainly, the battle indicates that any revolution against the established order, no matter how bloodless, will meet resistance.

In this chapter, the animals enrich their own history and add to the symbols of their victory. They already have the flag of the coming Republic of the Animals and their revolutionary anthem. To these they add military decorations, ceremonial artillery (Jones's shotgun) and, later, Major's skull (reminiscent of the embalmed body of Vladimir Lenin).

Key points

After the Rebellion, the animals destroy or change the symbols of their own oppression. They burn the crueller implements (whips, nose-rings, castrating knives, etc.), but reuse other items for their own purposes. For example, the medals given after the Battle of the Cowshed are old horse brasses (p.28), used to decorate carthorses during parades, but the 'ribbons with which the horses' manes and tails had usually been decorated on market days' are burnt, because 'animals should go naked' (p.13). Even the hawthorn planted on the sheep's grave represents this behaviour, because farmers largely used the Common Hawthorn for hedgerows, which serve as livestock barriers. The animals do not destroy everything belonging to the old regime if they can repurpose it.

Key vocabulary

Foxwood: The name of Pilkington's farm reflects his obsession with hunting.

Julius Caesar: Dictator of the Roman Empire (44–49 BC) and conqueror of Britain (55–54 BC), notable for his military successes and grasp of tactics.

Pinchfield: The name of Frederick's farm; suggests that he wrings as much money from the land as possible.

Stone: British imperial unit of measurement, equivalent to fourteen pounds. At fifteen stone, Snowball weighs just over ninety-five kilograms.

Thresh: To loosen the edible part of cereal grain from the inedible chaff. One traditional threshing method was to have heavy animals walk over the grain.

Q To what extent are the animals' icons (such as Major's skull) corrupted, banned, or destroyed in later chapters?

Chapter V (pp.30–39)

Summary: *Mollie leaves; Snowball plans to build a windmill but is exiled by Napoleon's secret police.*

This chapter is marked by continuing disagreements on farm policy between Napoleon and Snowball, most noticeably about the windmill (the central image of the second half of the novella).

- Snowball intends to electrify the farm, enabling 'fantastic machines which would do their work for them while they grazed at their ease in the fields or improved their minds with reading and conversation' (p.32).

- Snowball's theory of agriculture versus industry touches on Marx's idea that industrialisation split society in two: those who owned the means of production and those who did the work. Marx, with Frederick Engels, proposed that widespread technology would ease the burden on the peasantry and reduce capitalist cycles of over- and under-production of food.

- Napoleon, conversely, opposes the windmill on the grounds that 'the great need of the moment was to increase food production, and that if they wasted time on the windmill they would all starve to death' (p.33).

- Napoleon advocates maintaining the existing system, in which 'the farm was an old-fashioned one and had only the most primitive machinery' (p.32). In Napoleon's system, all work would continue to devolve onto the peasantry (the animals who are not pigs or dogs).

This chapter also foregrounds Napoleon's reliance on the secret police (the dogs) and propaganda. Napoleon's propagandists include Squealer, Minimus – the pig 'who had a remarkable gift for composing songs and poems' (p.38) – and the sheep. For example, the sheep start bleating 'Four legs good, two legs bad' at suspiciously apt moments: 'It was noticed that they were especially liable to break into "Four legs good, two legs bad" at crucial moments in Snowball's speeches' (p.32).

This is doubly significant:

- It prefigures the moment when Squealer teaches the sheep to bleat 'Four legs good, two legs *better!*' to support the newly bipedal (standing on two feet) pigs (p.89).

- It demonstrates the dangers in boiling a complex philosophy (such as Animalism) down to a simple maxim. Snowball originally did so because 'the stupider animals, such as the sheep, hens and ducks, were unable to learn the Seven Commandments by heart' (p.21), but the shortened version is easier to manipulate into an anti-Animalism philosophy.

Key vocabulary

Forelock: Part of a horse's mane growing over its forehead. 'Tugging the forelock' also means a salute given by a person to someone more powerful (particularly a working-class man to the local authority figure). Early in the novella, Mollie is described as having red ribbons plaited into her mane (p.3). After she flees the farm, she is described as having a red ribbon specifically around her forelock (p.31). Orwell may be playing with the association between the forelock and subservience (into which Mollie willingly enters).

'Napoleon is always right': 'Mussolini ha sempre ragione' ('Mussolini is always right') was a famous Italian Fascist propaganda slogan, and the last commandment in the 1938 edition of Mussolini's 'Fascist Decalogue' (sometimes translated as the 'Ten Commandments').

One Thousand Useful Things to Do About the House, Every Man His Own Bricklayer *and* Electricity for Beginners: Electricity for Beginners (1930) is a real book by Edward Harper Thomas. The others are probably also real, though no specific information on them can be found. Based on the titles, they are introductory works, ideally suited to someone with little prior technical knowledge.

Q Why does Napoleon drive Snowball from the farm?

Chapter VI (pp.40–48)

Summary: *The windmill is built and destroyed; the pigs sleep in the farmhouse and Napoleon trades with neighbouring farms.*

The first windmill is both built and destroyed in this chapter.

- The animals work significantly harder (and those who avoid the 'voluntary' work are punished with reduced rations) under Napoleon than they did in the early stages of the Rebellion, but are still happy in their work.

- Napoleon abandons his stated plans for increased food production: this season's harvest is less successful than the last and the ploughing is not completed in time for winter planting so, 'It was possible to foresee that the coming winter would be a hard one' (p.40).

- Allegorical readings sometimes link the failure of the first windmill to the failure of Stalin's first Five Year Plan (1928–33). The Five Year Plans (thirteen in total, between 1928 and 1991) were pushes for rapid economic development in the USSR. The first Five Year Plan involved combining small farms into large-scale collective farms, helping to transform Russia from a peasant-based agrarian (agricultural) economy to a leading industrial nation, but was also one of the causes of the 1932 famine, which killed millions. Certainly, the animals on Animal Farm face a 'bitter winter' in which they are 'always cold, and usually hungry as well' (p.49) because of the destroyed windmill and neglected harvest.

Under Napoleon's control, the farm rapidly returns to a capitalist system:

- Despite the animals' discomfort, he institutes trade with the neighbouring farms (p.42).

- Regarding trade, he announces that he 'intended to take the whole burden upon his own shoulders' (p.43). Ostensibly, he may appear to be saving the other animals from extra work, but this is actually a return to the division of labour that Marx deplored (the division described in the analysis of Chapter V): the animals work and Napoleon sells the produce.

- The pigs' decision to move into the farmhouse because it is 'more suited to the dignity of the Leader... to live in a house than in a mere sty' (p.45) also separates the ruling class (pigs and dogs) and the working classes (the other animals).

For the treatment of Snowball as a bogeyman, see analysis of Chapter VII.

Key vocabulary

Leader: 'Leader' is a common English translation of the German *Führer*, a title most closely associated with Adolf Hitler. (While previous party leaders had been called *Führer*, the name of their party was always appended to the title. Only Hitler was called *Führer* without further qualification.)

Q How does the building of the windmill reveal weaknesses in the farm's government?

Chapter VII (pp.49–60)

Summary: *The animals rebuild the windmill; Napoleon sells the hens' eggs, holds show trials, slaughters 'guilty' animals, and bans 'Beasts of England'.*

Snowball's position as bogeyman escalates in this chapter, to the point that 'Whenever anything went wrong it became usual to attribute it to Snowball' (p.52).

- A bogeyman is an imaginary figure that frightens children into better behaviour. 'Bogeyman' is also a general term for any threat used to keep people in line.

- Snowball is actually the second bogeyman with which the pigs frighten the other animals: Squealer repeatedly insists that Jones will return unless the animals behave in a certain way.

- Snowball's position as a bogeyman recalls Leon Trotsky's role in later Soviet politics (for Trotsky, see **Characters & Relationships**).

- Napoleon's transformation of Snowball from comrade to bogeyman includes accusing him of collaboration, asserting that he 'has sold himself to Frederick of Pinchfield Farm' (p.53). Collaborationists co-operate with enemy forces against the interests of their own country. The term had particular significance at the time when Orwell was writing *Animal Farm*. One of Nazi Germany's methods of controlling a conquered country was to establish a collaborationist government, such as the Vichy government in France or Vidkun Quisling's government in Norway.

  Napoleon demonstrates his willingness to rule by terror in this chapter, in a series of show trials.

- The trials recall the Great Purge (1936–38), in which Russian courts tried, executed, or exiled Stalin's opponents, particularly Lenin's colleagues and Trotsky's supporters.

- The Russian trials were held in open court, attended by some Western observers (particularly the trials of former members of the Russian government). Since the defendants confessed, apparently voluntarily, the trials appeared fair: observers did not see the means, such as torture, by which such confessions were extorted.

- Napoleon also holds his trials publicly, and the victims confess openly to their crimes. Since the novella's narration in this passage is limited to the animals' perspective, the reader is positioned as an observer, not knowing if (or how) the confessions were extorted.

- For Boxer's role in the trials, see **Themes, Ideas & Values**.

Key points

'Beasts of England' is reminiscent of 'The Red Flag,' a protest song strongly associated with left-wing politics (especially socialism). Written by Jim Connell in 1889, 'The Red Flag' was originally sung to 'The White Cockade', a martial tune from the seventeenth-century Jacobite uprising in Great Britain. However, it came to be sung to the much slower German tune, 'O Tannenbaum' ('O Christmas Tree'), particularly after it was adopted as the official anthem of the British Labour Party. Many people, including Connell, were upset when the triumphant protest song became a melancholy dirge. The melancholy tune became apt, however, when the Labour Party proved to be pro-war during World War II, despite in-party opposition. 'Beasts of England' is originally sung to a loud, triumphant tune. After the show trials, Clover and the animals sing it 'very tunefully, but slowly and mournfully, in a way they had never sung it before' (p.59). Like 'The Red Flag,' 'Beasts of England' has two sides: both a spontaneous rebel song and the mournful anthem of a political system that is not what it promised to be.

Q What is the significance of the hens' protest?

Chapter VIII (pp.61–73)

Summary: Napoleon sells his lumber to Frederick for counterfeit bills; Frederick and his men blow up the completed windmill; the pigs discover alcohol.

The animals struggle to both rebuild the windmill and to maintain regular farm work. The second windmill, however, meets the same fate as the first.

* Some allegorical readings suggest that the destruction of the second windmill reflects the Nazi invasion of Russia in 1941. In this analysis, Frederick represents Adolf Hitler. However, be careful not to over-read this example. Frederick and Pilkington 'disliked each other so much that it was difficult for them to come to any agreement, even in defence of their own interests' (p.24). But Pilkington passively supports Frederick's invasion by refusing to come to the animals' aid (pp.68–69), which is not in keeping with his role in the last chapter (see analysis of Chapter X).

* Frederick is able to destroy the windmill because his technology is superior: half-a-dozen shotguns and gunpowder destroy two years of animal labour. The animals are still struggling (via the windmill) to move past an old-fashioned agrarian system to an industrialised economy. Until they do, they are vulnerable to any more-industrialised farms, even if those farms are not particularly rich (for example, Frederick's fifteen men have only six shotguns, rather than a shotgun each, but still overpower the animals).

This chapter also emphasises the pigs' increasing reliance on propaganda (see **Themes, Ideas & Values**).

Key vocabulary

Crown Derby: High-quality porcelain; display items rather than ordinary crockery. (Given the list of furnishings in Chapter II, they are likely the most expensive objects in the house.)

Q How do the sentiments expressed in 'Comrade Napoleon' contradict 'Beasts of England'?

Chapter IX (pp.74–84)

Summary: *The animals rebuild the windmill a third time; Napoleon again reduces rations, but builds a schoolhouse for his piglets; Boxer falls ill and the pigs send him to the knacker's yard.*

The central image in this chapter (and, perhaps, the entire novella) is Boxer's removal to the knacker's yard.

- Allegorical readings of the novella often identify Boxer with the proletariat (the working classes) as a whole or with the loyal Bolsheviks killed during the Great Purge. Boxer is certainly the most loyal of all the original rebels: 'His two slogans, "I will work harder" and "Napoleon is always right", seemed to him a sufficient answer to all problems' (p.41).

- The horror of Boxer's eventual fate is reinforced by his plans for his coming retirement, as promised in the original outline of Animalism: 'To tell you the truth I had been looking forward to my retirement. And perhaps, as Benjamin is growing old too, they will let him retire at the same time and be a companion to me' (p.80).

- The planned retirement is modest: 'it was rumoured that a corner of the large pasture was to be fenced off and turned into a grazing-ground for superannuated animals. For a horse, it was said, the pension would be five pounds of corn a day and, in winter, fifteen pounds of hay, with a carrot or possibly an apple on public holidays' (p.74). The complete disdain with which the pigs regard the other animals is evident in their unwillingness to provide even this little amount, when most of the farm's money goes towards the pigs' comfort (p.76).

- Boxer's last appearance in the novella reinforces what he has sacrificed for the good of Animal Farm: 'there was the sound of a tremendous drumming of hoofs inside the van. He was trying to kick his way out. The time had been when a few kicks from Boxer's hoofs would have smashed the van to matchwood. But alas! his strength had left him; and in a few moments the sound of drumming hoofs grew fainter and died away' (p.82).

- The final comment on Boxer's fate is perhaps the most caustic line in the entire novella: 'And the word went round that from somewhere or other the pigs had acquired the money to buy themselves another case of whisky' (p.84).

Key vocabulary

Knacker: Someone who processes animals considered unfit for human consumption (frequently horses too old to continue work), turning them into such products as dog food and glue. A knacker's yard differs from a slaughterhouse, in which animals are slaughtered for human consumption.

Matchwood: In this context, wood that has been splintered into small pieces under impact.

Q Why do the animals not react more strongly to Boxer's fate?

Chapter X (pp.85–95)

Summary: *The farm becomes richer and the animals poorer; the pigs walk upright and wear clothes; Napoleon invites neighbouring farmers to tour the farm; the animals can no longer tell pig from man.*

After the startling moment in which the pigs appear walking upright, it 'did not seem strange' (p.90) when the pigs adopt human clothes. But the clothes, particularly Napoleon's 'ratcatcher breeches' (p.90) break more than just the third commandment of Animalism.

'Ratcatcher' is a general term for attire (usually tweed) worn for fox-hunting, especially during the less formal cub-hunting season in the autumn. Napoleon's adoption of hunting attire has dual significance:

- Fox-hunting is an upper-class sport, though Mr Jones's possession of ratcatcher breeches suggests that he, like many farmers, supports hunting and regards foxes as vermin. Napoleon's attire is therefore a strong rejection of the socialist principles of early Animalism.

- Fox-hunting is widely criticised on humanitarian grounds, not only because of the way the fox is killed at the conclusion of the hunt but also because foxhounds are often euthanised when they can no longer work. Foxhounds are often fed on horsemeat, normally that of old horses who can no longer work, such as Boxer. When Major warns Boxer of his fate, for example, he specifically mentions that the knacker will 'boil you down for the foxhounds' (p.5). Thus, in wearing the ratcatcher breeches, Napoleon is also breaking the sixth commandment of Animalism ('No animal shall kill any other animal') in spirit if not (at this moment) in practice.

The meeting between the pigs and the men in this chapter is a version of the Tehran Conference (28 November–1 December 1943), a meeting between Joseph Stalin, Franklin D Roosevelt and Winston Churchill to plan future offensives against Germany. It was the first such meeting, since Stalin had not attended earlier conferences. Concessions made to Stalin during the Tehran Conference are often cited as one of the catalysts for the Cold War.

In his introduction to the Ukrainian edition, Orwell wrote:

> A number of readers may finish the book with the impression that it ends in the complete reconciliation of the pigs and the humans. That was not my intention; on the contrary I meant it to end on a loud note of discord, for I wrote it immediately after the Teheran [sic] Conference, which everybody thought had established the best possible relations between the USSR and the West. I personally did not believe that such good relations would last long; and as events have shown, I wasn't far wrong.

Key points

The pigs' reading material is all real. *John Bull* (1820–1957) was a strongly patriotic weekly London periodical, as suggested by the title: John Bull is a personification of Great Britain, presented as a minor landholder ('yeoman'). *Tit-Bits* (1881–1984) was a mass-market weekly magazine, focusing on dramatic, sensational human-interest stories. The *Daily Mirror* (1903–present day) is a tabloid newspaper; it later became strongly left wing, but was originally a conservative, middle-class paper. Napoleon's newspapers recall Jones falling asleep over the *News of the World*, another conservative newspaper, in Chapter II.

Key vocabulary

Watered silk: Silk treated to produce a wavy effect (also called 'moire'). Mrs Jones only wears the delicate dress on Sundays, a day when she doesn't work.

Wireless: Archaic British term for radio.

Q How do the 'short animal lives' affect how Orwell tells the story?

Q What does Pilkington mean when he refers to the working classes?

CHARACTERS & RELATIONSHIPS

Animals

Napoleon

Key quotes

'Napoleon was a large, rather fierce-looking Berkshire boar, the only Berkshire on the farm, not much of a talker but with a reputation for getting his own way.' (p.9)

'It had become usual to give Napoleon the credit for every successful achievement and every stroke of good fortune.' (p.62)

Napoleon – the pig who first rebels against Jones and then becomes Jones – is the primary antagonist of *Animal Farm*, though he rarely takes action himself, preferring to act through proxies. He is a Berkshire boar, an un-castrated pig being bred by Jones for sale (p.9). Since Berkshires (an extremely old and now extremely rare breed of pig) were bred as pork producers, Napoleon has a vested interest in rebelling against Jones and saving himself from slaughter.

But Napoleon's attack on Snowball also shows that he is deeply attracted to personal power. He has no public-spirited reason to exile his rival: the farm is operating well enough under Snowball's leadership. He does not, whatever his propagandists claim, act in the animals' best interests: his actions derive from his desire for absolute power and show his strong contempt for all animals other than pigs.

Napoleon bears the name of the French dictator Napoleon Bonaparte, but is based, at least partly, on Joseph Stalin. Peter Davison's introduction to the 1989 Penguin edition, for example, quotes Orwell as saying that this is his novella 'contre Stalin' (*contre*, a French preposition, means 'against'). Napoleon's rise to power on the farm shows strong similarities to the period prior to World War II, in which Stalin consolidated his position of power (c. 1927–39). Stalin worked to bolster the scope and power of his secret police, just as Napoleon does through the agency of his fierce (and fiercely loyal) dogs. Stalin also held long-running and wide-ranging purges of political opponents (collectively called the Great Purge), just as Napoleon does (pp.55–57).

Most tellingly, Napoleon, like Stalin, bases his power on a cult of personality: the creation of a heroic, idealised public image, built up through excessive praise and frequent tribute. In Stalin's case, this included naming multiple towns and cities after him, granting him exaggerated titles, and making him the focus of artistic and literary endeavours. After the purges on Animal Farm, Napoleon demonstrates these same tendencies: he appears in public 'attended not only by his retinue of dogs but by a black cockerel who marched in front of him and acted as a kind of trumpeter' (p.62); the pigs grant him 'such titles as Father of All Animals, Terror of Mankind, Protector of the Sheepfold, Ducklings' Friend, and the like' (p.62); and Minimus writes poems praising Napoleon, which are then inscribed on the barn wall, 'surmounted by a portrait of Napoleon, in profile' (p.63). This cult of personality is balanced against the simultaneous demonisation of Snowball. Napoleon's power is based not on the pig himself, but on a carefully constructed, maintained and idealised image of the pig.

However, Napoleon is not entirely without positive characteristics: Peter Davison points out that Orwell rewrote the destruction of the second windmill to say that 'all the animals, except Napoleon, flung themselves flat on their bellies and hid their faces' (p.69), acknowledging Stalin's bravery in staying in Moscow as the German army advanced.

Snowball

Key quotes

'Snowball was a more vivacious pig than Napoleon, quicker in speech and more inventive, but was not considered to have the same depth of character.' (p.9)

'Until now the animals had been about equally divided in their sympathies, but in a moment Snowball's eloquence had carried them away.' (p.35)

Snowball, like Napoleon and Squealer, is one of the ringleaders of the Rebellion. He is active in developing Animalism (pp.9–10), constructing and interpreting the Seven Commandments (pp.21–22), and designing the symbols of the Rebellion, such as the Animal Farm flag (p.19).

Snowball's early activities all focus on improving the welfare of the farm animals. His 'Animal Committees' (p.20) are largely unsuccessful, but the reasons behind their failure are not clear. For example, the Wild Comrades' Re-education Committee fails: the wild animals 'continued to behave very much as before, and when treated with generosity simply took advantage of it' (p.20). But it is unclear whether the plan is badly constructed or badly applied: the cat, for example, is active in this committee but for purely self-interested reasons (p.20). Some of Snowball's plans are effective: the windmill is practical and the animals' literacy is improved.

Though Snowball does work for the good of the farm, he is not entirely selfless: he is complicit in the retaining of milk and apples for the sole consumption of the pigs (pp.22–23). Whether Snowball would have proved as corrupt as Napoleon is unanswerable. His expulsion, though, has two advantages for Napoleon: it grants him absolute control and provides him with a bogeyman on whom he can blame all Animal Farm's problems.

Allegorical readings suggest that Snowball is based, at least partly, on Leon Trotsky (1879–1940), one of the leaders of the 1917 Russian Revolution, second only in power to Vladimir Lenin. After Lenin's death in 1924, Trotsky was sidelined as Stalin's power increased, before he was exiled from Russia (in 1929), sentenced to death in absentia (in 1936), and assassinated in Mexico (in 1940). After his exile, Trotsky was treated in propaganda as a malevolent bogeyman whose aim was the destruction of Soviet Russia: the show trials of the Grand Purge, for example, were ostensibly aimed at removing Trotskyite conspirators.

Squealer

Key quotes

'The others said of Squealer that he could turn black into white.' (p.9)

Squealer is the third member of the group of pigs who develop Animalism. Unlike Napoleon, he is a 'porker' (p.9), a castrated boar. Despite his role in formulating Animalism, Squealer is not particularly dominant in the early stages of the novella: he is overshadowed by the more dynamic figures of Napoleon and Snowball and by their constant disagreements. After Snowball's expulsion, Squealer's power increases, but he remains Napoleon's devoted lieutenant, never his equal in power. He prospers under Napoleon; by the end of the novella, he 'was so fat that he could with difficulty see out of his eyes' (p.85).

Squealer acts as Napoleon's mouthpiece; once Napoleon removes himself from public appearances, 'he did not even appear on Sunday mornings, but issued his orders through one of the other pigs, usually Squealer' (p.50). More significantly, he acts as Napoleon's chief propagandist, using his persuasive speech to convince the other animals that 'everything was getting better and better' (p.87). As the animals grow older and their memories grow dimmer, Squealer's propaganda becomes more real to them than their own experiences. (See 'Propaganda' under **Themes, Ideas & Values** for details.)

Allegorical readings suggest that Squealer is based on Vyascheslav Molotov (1890–1986), Stalin's protégé, premier of Russia (1930–41) and Minister for Foreign Affairs (1939–49). In the latter position he gave his name and his signature to the Molotov–Ribbentrop Pact, the 1939 treaty of non-aggression between Russia and Nazi Germany. Molotov was deeply loyal to Stalin throughout the former's period of power; for example, he signed numerous execution lists during the Great Purge without question. Molotov fell out of favour after World War II, but nonetheless survived Stalin.

Boxer

Key quotes

'Boxer was the admiration of everybody. He had been a hard worker even in Jones's time, but now he seemed more like three horses than one; there were days when the entire work of the farm seemed to rest upon his mighty shoulders.' (p.18)

'A white stripe down his nose gave him a somewhat stupid appearance, and in fact he was not of first-rate intelligence, but he was universally respected for his steadiness of character and tremendous powers of work.' (p.2)

Boxer is the character who most ardently believes in the Rebellion. Like Clover, he is called a 'cart-horse': some (unspecified) breed of draft horse – extremely large and heavy horses designed for difficult, arduous physical labour, particularly ploughing or other forms of farm labour. His strength comes from his great size: horses are measured to the withers (where the neck meets the back), so at almost eighteen hands (see **Key Vocabulary** for Chapter II), Boxer stands nearly six feet high (around 182 centimetres) at his withers. Including his head and neck, he towers over not only the other animals, but also the humans. When he rises up on his hind legs in the Battle of the Cowshed, he is easily able to strike the stable-lad on the top of the head (p.27).

Because they work closely with humans, draft horses are bred to be extremely strong, patient and docile, all characteristics that Boxer displays in the novella. Despite his great size and strength, Boxer is gentle, as when he steps carefully across the barn to avoid injuring smaller animals (p.2) or when he mourns the stableboy he believes he's killed at the Battle of the Cowshed: '"I have no wish to take life, not even human life," repeated Boxer, and his eyes were full of tears' (p.28). He strives constantly for self-improvement: he intends 'to devote the rest of his life to learning the remaining twenty-two letters of the alphabet' (p.81); and 'His answer to every problem, every setback, was "I will work harder!" – which he had adapted as his personal motto' (p.18).

Boxer also has a streak of martyrdom. He regularly works longer hours, goes without sleep and undertakes voluntary extra work. Furthermore, when Snowball declares that 'All animals should go naked', Boxer 'fetched the small straw hat which he wore in summer to keep the flies out of his ears, and flung it onto the fire with the rest' (p.13), even though horses' ears are highly sensitive, and fly bites can cause irritation, bleeding, and infection. Boxer's self-sacrificial impulses cause his ill health: he grows increasingly gaunt, until Clover and Benjamin warn him to take care of his health, 'He did not care what happened so long as a good store of stone was accumulated before he went on pension' (p.79). And it is Boxer's total devotion to the Rebellion that allows the pigs to discard him as they do; except for one moment when he questions the anti-Snowball propaganda (p.55), Boxer never ceases to believe that the pigs have the animals' best interests at heart or that they will care for him when he has given his strength and health to the cause. As such, the moment when Boxer is taken to the knacker's is perhaps the most emotionally devastating moment in the novella.

Benjamin

Key quotes

'Benjamin was the oldest animal on the farm, and the worst tempered.' (p.2)

'Old Benjamin, the donkey, seemed quite unchanged since the Rebellion. He did his work in the same slow obstinate way as he had done it in Jones's time, never shirking and never volunteering for extra work either.' (p.19)

Benjamin is the one sardonic (scornful, sarcastic), critical inhabitant of Animal Farm, persistently refusing to express interest in or excitement about the Rebellion. When the other animals question him on the subject, he replies, 'Donkeys live a long time. None of you has ever seen a dead donkey' (p.19). By this comment – which evokes the colloquial phrase 'donkey's years', meaning an extremely long time – Benjamin underscores his lack of faith that the Rebellion will bring about any change. He is among the more intelligent animals: he 'could read as well as any pig, but never exercised his faculty. So far as he knew, he said, there was nothing worth reading' (p.21). He is a silent and morose character: 'Alone among the animals on the farm he never laughed. If asked why, he would say that he saw nothing to laugh at' (p.2).

The one soft spot in Benjamin's personality is his unspoken devotion to Boxer: 'the two of them usually spent their Sundays together in the small paddock beyond the orchard, grazing side by side and never speaking' (p.2). After Boxer's injury, it is Benjamin who, with Clover, keeps Boxer company in his stall for the last two days of his life (pp.80–81). His devotion is returned; the injured Boxer hopes that 'perhaps, as Benjamin is growing old too, they will let him retire at the same time and be a companion to me' (p.80). Consequently, the only time we see Benjamin's sardonic facade crack is when Boxer is taken to the knacker's (p.81).

Donkeys are frequently cited in proverbs and derogatory phrases, usually as examples of lack of intelligence (as in 'donkey work' for dull, repetitive tasks) or stubbornness (as in the adjective 'asinine,' from 'ass,' an alternative name for donkey). While Benjamin is clearly intelligent, he does show the stereotypical donkey traits of stubbornness and natural wariness.

Clover

Key quotes

'Clover was a stout, motherly mare, approaching middle life, who had never got her figure back after her fourth foal.' (p.2)

'If she herself had any picture of the future, it had been of a society of animals set free from hunger and the whip, all equal, each working according to his capacity, the strong protecting the weak, as she had protected the lost brood of ducklings with her foreleg on the night of Major's speech.' (p.58)

Like her fellow carthorse Boxer, Clover is a faithful disciple of Animalism from the earliest days:

> These two had great difficulty in thinking anything out for themselves, but having once accepted the pigs as their teachers they absorbed everything that they were told, and passed it on to the other animals by simple arguments (p.11).

Clover is rather more intelligent than Boxer: while he can only read the letters A to D, 'Clover learnt the whole alphabet, but could not put words together' (p.21). However, she lacks the self-sacrificial impulse that drives Boxer to work himself to death. Furthermore, as conditions on Animal Farm worsen, Clover adopts a more questioning stance than Boxer does. For example, when the pigs move into the farmhouse,

> Boxer passed it off as usual with 'Napoleon is always right!', but Clover, who thought she remembered a definite ruling against beds, went to the end of the barn and tried to puzzle out the Seven Commandments which were inscribed there (p.45).

Clover's questions do not mean that she rejects Animalism; on the contrary, she remains devoted to the principles of the Rebellion even when Napoleon's rule extends to the horrors of show trials and executions:

> There was no thought of rebellion or disobedience in her mind. She knew that even as things were they were far better off than

they had been in the days of Jones ... Whatever happened, she
would remain faithful, work hard, carry out the orders that were
given to her, and accept the leadership of Napoleon (pp.58–59).

Clover's dominant characteristic is her motherliness, as when she
shelters the ducklings from harm (p.2), comforts the injured Boxer
(pp.80–81), and instructs the new animals in the principles of Animalism
until they come to regard her with 'an almost filial respect' (p.86). This
motherliness also underscores Clover's faith in Animalism; under Jones's
rule, as old Major points out, the 'four foals you bore, who should have
been the support and pleasure of your old age' were all sold once they
were a year old: 'you will never see one of them again' (p.4). Clover
continues to believe that life is better under Napoleon's rule than under
Jones', though it is through her 'old dim eyes' that we see that there is
little difference between the two (p.94).

Major
Major is the Middle White boar who incites the animals to rebel. Middle
White pigs (like Berkshires) were pork producers, so Major is well aware
that he is 'one of the lucky ones' (p.5) – as a show pig and then a breeding
boar, he has been protected from slaughter. He is twelve years old (a
venerable age for a domestic pig), with over 400 children and a position
of authority among the farm animals. Now stout, he is 'still a majestic-
looking pig, with a wise and benevolent appearance in spite of the fact
that his tushes had never been cut' (p.1). Major dies in Chapter II, but
has already given the other animals the basic structure of Animalism.
Allegorical readings suggest that Major is partly a composite of two men:
Karl Marx (1818–83), German philosopher and political theorist – who,
along with Friedrich Engels, wrote *The Communist Manifesto* (1848)
– and Vladimir Ilyich Lenin (1870–1924), leader of the 1917 October
Revolution and first leader of Soviet Russia.

Key points
Although the characters in *Animal Farm* are often based on historical personages,
the allegorical connections can be overemphasised. For example, old Major the
boar sounds like Karl Marx and is venerated like Vladimir Lenin. But he is also a
character with his own specific back-story, in his exposure to seditious ideas as a

young piglet and then his unusually long life as a show pig. Both of these influence his ideas about Animalism. If characters are read exclusively as allegorical versions of historical figures, readers might miss important points in the fiction that don't relate to those real-life personalities.

Humans

Mr Jones

Jones is the owner of Manor Farm before the Rebellion. He is 'a hard master' (p.11), but before the events of the novella he was also 'a capable farmer' (p.11). These two traits combined suggest that he worked his animals hard but at least took sufficient care of them to ensure that they could continue to work hard. However, he has ceased to be a good farmer some time before the novella begins: 'He had become much disheartened after losing money in a lawsuit, and had taken to drinking more than was good for him' (p.11). Consequently, the farm is neglected, the farm workers become lazy and the animals become hungry. After the Rebellion, Jones manages to garner support from his neighbours (p.24), but loses their sympathy after the Battle of the Cowshed. He then moves to another part of the country and dies in an 'inebriates' home' (p.85) from the after-effects of his drinking.

Mr Whymper

Napoleon's agent, hired to trade with neighbouring farms, is a solicitor from the nearby village. His involvement allows Napoleon to maintain the illusion that the animals are not breaking the resolutions: 'Never to have any dealings with human beings, never to engage in trade, never to make use of money' (p.43). Whymper also unwittingly spreads propaganda for the pigs – the Animal Farm that he sees (for example, when Napoleon shows him the doctored grain bins in the store-shed (p.50)) and that he talks about in the village is not an accurate reflection of conditions on the farm. Whymper is 'a sly-looking little man' and not a successful solicitor: he is only 'in a very small way of business' (p.44). He is clever enough to realise that the animals will need human assistance and to make himself available (p.44), but he's an inefficient broker: he doesn't seem to be aware, for example, that Frederick's banknotes are counterfeit (pp.67–68) .

Mr Pilkington

An 'easy-going gentleman farmer' (p.24), Pilkington farms because
it allows him to hunt and fish. Pilkington's Foxwood Farm adjoins
Animal Farm, making Pilkington anxious about the consequences of the
Rebellion. Like Frederick, he is willing to enter into trade negotiations
with Napoleon (p.63). Unlike Frederick, he is not inspired to actively
attack Animal Farm, but nor is he willing to come to Napoleon's aid
(pp.68–69). Though Pilkington is one of the 'deputation of neighbouring
farmers [who] had been invited to make a tour of inspection' (p.90–91)
in the final chapter and gives a toast in which he emphasises 'the friendly
feelings that subsisted, and ought to subsist, between Animal Farm and
its neighbours' (p.92), he ends the novella in the midst of a bitter quarrel
with Napoleon (p.95).

Mr Frederick

Animal Farm's other neighbour, Frederick is a 'tough, shrewd man'. His
farm, Pinchfield, is better run than Pilkington's farm, but Frederick is
'perpetually involved in lawsuits' and known for 'driving hard bargains'
(p.24). The first trait suggests that Frederick may be the man against whom
Jones lost his lawsuit, prompting his alcoholism and neglect of Manor
Farm. The second trait prefigures the moment when Frederick cheats
Napoleon out of his lumber by paying for it with counterfeit banknotes
(pp.67–68). Unlike Pilkington, Frederick is active in his hatred of Animal
Farm, leading his men in a successful attack on the windmill (p.69).
Though the animals ultimately rout (overthrow) Frederick and his men,
his attack costs them two years' work during which they neglect the
general running of the farm. It seems unlikely that Napoleon will come to
peaceful terms with Frederick: Frederick is not, for example, mentioned
as a member of the 'deputation of neighbouring farmers' (pp.90–91)
whom Napoleon invites to inspect the farm.

THEMES, IDEAS & VALUES

Socialism vs. Totalitarianism

Key quotes

'No one believes more firmly than Comrade Napoleon that all animals are equal. He would be only too happy to let you make your decisions for yourselves. But sometimes you might make the wrong decisions, comrades, and then where should we be?' (p.37)

'Napoleon had denounced such ideas as contrary to the spirit of Animalism. The truest happiness, he said, lay in working hard and living frugally.' (p.86)

Orwell's essay 'Why I Write' encapsulates his attitude to his work shortly after *Animal Farm* first appeared in print: 'Every line of serious work I have written since 1936 has been written, directly or indirectly, *against* totalitarianism and *for* democratic socialism, as I understand it' (Orwell, 2004, p.8).

'Socialism' and 'communism' are not interchangeable terms, though they do share some common ground. Socialism is based on the concept of equal power, shared ownership and the elimination of hierarchical government. Animalism, as it is set out in the days before the Rebellion, is a socialist philosophy. Old Major establishes this when he says, 'among us animals let there be perfect unity, perfect comradeship in the struggle. All men are enemies. All animals are comrades' (p.6). To put it more simply, 'All animals are equal' (p.15). In the early days of the Rebellion, equality is not an abstract concept: there is no single level of work, for example, to which all animals aspire. Rather, 'everyone worked according to his capacity' (p.18). In the utopia that the animals hope to establish, the state cares equally for all and everyone works as hard as possible to perpetuate the wealth from which all benefit.

This model is effective in the early months. The animals 'finished the harvest in two days less time than it had usually taken Jones and his men' and 'it was the biggest harvest that the farm had ever seen' (p.17). Though the work is difficult for the sometimes inexperienced animals, food is plentiful and they still have time for leisure (p.18). Animalism, the animals' socialist philosophy, is successful at the first trial. But the seeds of the coming corruption are evident even here, as the pigs claim specific benefits for themselves, as 'brainworkers' (p.23).

Though Orwell is drawing in part on Soviet Russia for his allegory, the corrupted form of government that slowly overtakes Animal Farm is not communism. Indeed, the defining characteristic of Napoleon's rule is the extent to which he openly and deliberately rewrites the precepts of Animalism. Critics who read the novella seeking specific parallels with Soviet Russia often tend to overlook this aspect of the book. As Robert Pearce puts it:

> But there is one issue in the book for which there seems no real-life equivalent: this is the rewriting of the original revolutionary aims, the principles of Animalism. Admittedly revolutionary idealism in Russia and elsewhere was betrayed and perverted, but there was no outward repudiation of Marxist rhetoric (Pearce, 1998, p.66).

Napoleon's increasing power is based on a clear, open repudiation of Animalism. When he works against principles that were discussed but never put in writing, he relies on Squealer's persuasiveness and the suggestibility of the animals. For example, when he initiates trade with other farms and the animals object, Squealer points out that nothing has been written against it: 'And since it was certainly true that nothing of the kind existed in writing, the animals were satisfied that they had been mistaken' (p.44). But even when his plans contradict one of the Seven Commandments, Napoleon has no qualms about not only breaking the commandment but also physically rewriting it (e.g. p.73).

What results is a totalitarian state. Totalitarianism is a political system in which the state (often a single leader) has unlimited authority, ordinary citizens have little to no share in decision-making, and both private and public life are regulated by the state. Totalitarianism is the antithesis of socialism, but can itself be either left wing or right wing, communist (as with Stalin) or fascist (as with Hitler). Napoleon's totalitarianism is not an outgrowth of Animalism, but rather an expression of his individual desire for power and an evocation of the corrupting ability of power.

Around the time that he was writing *Animal Farm*, Orwell wrote that 'Socialists don't claim to be able to make the world perfect: they claim to be able to make it better' (cited by Williams 2007, p.110). In *Animal Farm*, Orwell argues that socialism can make the world better, albeit temporarily, just as he argues that totalitarianism leads to a world of lies, secrets and terror.

Key points

Orwell's insistence that his work is '*against* totalitarianism and *for* democratic socialism' is central to Orwellian scholarship. Some critics ignore 'for democratic socialism', implicitly arguing that 'against totalitarianism' is of more importance to Orwell's philosophy. However, both parts of the quotation are equally important: it is not solely a question of what Orwell was against, but also a question of what he was for.

Corruption

Key quotes

'All animals are equal.' (p.15)

'ALL ANIMALS ARE EQUAL, BUT SOME ANIMALS ARE MORE EQUAL THAN OTHERS.' (p.90)

The animals' revolution becomes corrupted, but is itself born out of corrupted power. Mr Jones has absolute power over the animals on his farm: not only to work them as hard as he likes and feed them as little as he likes, but to entirely control their lives and deaths. Because of *Animal Farm*'s allegorical connection to Soviet Russia, Jones can be read as a representation of Tsar Nicholas II, the last in a line of absolute monarchs. But in a novella written during the great clash of totalitarian powers in Europe and beyond (see **Background & Context**), he is a symbol of any totalitarian leader.

However, as old Major points out in his speech, Man is always totalitarian in his relations with animals: 'There, comrades, is the answer to all our problems. It is summed up in a single word – Man' (p.4). Major's use of the symbolic, singular 'Man' (rather than 'men' or even 'Jones') reinforces the argument that Jones's totalitarian control over the animals is part of a broader problem, not unique to the farmer himself. Jones's specific problem is that he has become corrupted. In his legal disappointments and resultant drunkenness, he has forgotten that his power is a stewardship and he must care for his animals' welfare even as he exploits their labour. He deputises the actual work to 'idle and dishonest' farm workers and spends his own time 'reading the newspapers, drinking, and occasionally feeding Moses', his tame raven (p.11). Corrupt, decadent, and idle, he creates the conditions for his own overthrow.

In Jones's place, the animals establish a socialist system. Even the pigs are involved in the hard labour of the first harvest, as Boxer and Clover 'tramp steadily round and round the field with a pig walking behind and calling out "Gee up, comrade!" or "Whoa back, comrade!" as the case might be' (p.17). But the seeds of the coming corruption are evident from the day after the Rebellion, when the animals look with 'considerable interest' at the fresh milk:

> 'Never mind the milk, comrades!' cried Napoleon, placing himself in front of the buckets. 'That will be attended to. The harvest is more important ... So the animals trooped down to the hayfield to begin the harvest, and when they came back in the evening it was noticed that the milk had disappeared (p.16).

The pigs' claim to the fresh milk is rapidly extended to the windfall apples; the animals 'had assumed as a matter of course that these would be shared out equally' (p.22).

Except for those first buckets of milk, the pigs make no attempt to hide the fact that they are claiming particular advantages for themselves. They claim the windfall apples quite openly: 'the order went forth that all the windfall apples were to be collected and brought to the harness-room for the use of the pigs' (p.22). The incident with the apples is, in fact, the first use of a technique that later serves the pigs well: the use of spurious (false) evidence to support the pigs' increasing power. In this case, Squealer claims, 'Milk and apples (this has been proved by Science, comrades) contain substances absolutely necessary to the well-being of a pig' (p.23).

Orwell described this moment as the 'turning-point of the story', not simply because of the abuse of power, but because the abuse occurs openly and with the animals' agreement. In the introduction to the 1989 Penguin edition of the novella, Orwell is quoted as writing to a friend that:

> I meant the moral to be that revolutions only effect a radical improvement when the masses are alert and know how to chuck their leaders out as soon as the latter have done their job (p.vii).

The corruption that follows on from the pigs' appropriation of the milk and apples is, then, partly the result of the other animals' willingness to accept these small changes. Leaders, suggests Orwell, will always take these small privileges for themselves. But the openness with which the privileges are claimed gives the other animals the opportunity to protest. The fact that they accept the spurious claims – by which the pigs justify these small privileges – leads to large privileges, to a sharp division between labourers and the ruling class of pigs and dogs, to show trials, secrets, and terror. In *Animal Farm*, Orwell argues that corruption is generated not only by the corrupt leaders themselves but also by the failure of others to recognise it and to stem it at its source.

Loyalty

Key quotes

'I do not understand it. I would not have believed that such things could happen on our farm. It must be due to some fault in ourselves.' (p.57)

'There was no thought of rebellion or disobedience in her mind. She knew that even as things were they were far better off than they had been in the days of Jones ...' (pp.58–59)

One reason why the corruption on Animal Farm continues unchecked is the animals' great loyalty to the farm itself and to the principles of Animalism. Such loyalty is encapsulated in the quote from Boxer (above, p.57) after the show trials, in which he places the blame for the terror not on Napoleon but on the other animals themselves.

Indeed, Boxer is the epitome (embodiment) of loyalty in the novella. Clover and Boxer are the loyal adherents of Animalism, the ones who were 'unfailing in their attendance at the secret meetings in the barn, and led the singing of "Beasts of England"' (p.11). Clover never rebels against the principles of Animalism, not even in thought. But she asks Muriel to read the commandments for her, when the pigs' behaviour seems to contravene them (e.g. p.45) and she questions the reasons behind the show trials (p.58).

Boxer never questions the pigs' loyalty to Animalism. The only time he even vaguely wavers from this stance is when Squealer declares that Snowball had always been Jones's agent. Boxer's slight uneasiness, his declaration that 'I believe that at the Battle of the Cowshed he was a good comrade' (p.55), is easily overridden by Squealer's rebuttal. But even this slight faltering in loyalty is destined for punishment. Squealer 'cast a very ugly look at Boxer with his little twinkling eyes' (p.55).

The animals never connect Boxer's brief moment of doubt to the dogs' attack: they assume that the reason the dogs 'appeared to go quite mad' (p.56) is because they have tasted blood. More specifically, Boxer never connects the two events. Even when he has the dog under his hoof, he 'looked to Napoleon to know whether he should crush the dog to death or let it go' (p.56).

Boxer's loyalty is as responsible for his death as the pigs' corruption is. Certainly, the pigs only value the other animals in terms of profit. But Boxer's unshakeable loyalty is what drives him to work himself to death. In Morris Dickstein's words, Boxer's 'innocent faith in the new order enables it to use him up and throw him away' (Dickstein, 2007, p.143). The fact that Boxer's faith contributes to his death does not mean that he deserves the pigs' betrayal. But it does suggest that Clover's scepticism is perhaps a better solution to living in a corrupt political system.

In the end, the animals adopt a model that is closer to Clover's scepticism than to Boxer's unquestioning faith. As the farm expands and prospers, other animals join in – animals who never participated in the Rebellion. The original animals tell them stories of 'the old heroic days, the expulsion of Jones, the writing of the Seven Commandments, the great battles in which the human invaders had been defeated' (p.88). The further the farm moves from those commandments, the more subversive this behaviour is. And the animals are conscious of this:

Even the tune of 'Beasts of England' was perhaps hummed secretly here and there: at any rate it was a fact that every animal on the farm knew it, though no one would have dared sing it aloud. It might be that their lives were hard and not all of their hopes had been fulfilled; but they were conscious that they were not as other animals (p.88).

The animals retain their loyalty to the ideals for which they originally fought. But after the pigs' most loyal supporter, Boxer, is destroyed when his usefulness comes to an end, their loyalty is tempered. By singing the forbidden song, they show that their loyalty is not always to the pigs' dictates, but to something that never came to pass: Animalism and the chance for a better existence.

Religion

Key quotes

'In Sugarcandy Mountain it was Sunday seven days a week, clover was in season all year round, and lump sugar and linseed cakes grew on the hedges.' (pp.10–11)

'"Up there, comrades," he would say solemnly, pointing to the sky with his large beak – "up there, just on the other side of that dark cloud that you can see – there it lies, Sugarcandy Mountain ..."' (p.78)

The primary image of religion in *Animal Farm* is the concept of 'Sugarcandy Mountain,' a paradise-like afterlife for animals. It is described, appropriately, by Moses the raven (Jones's pet). Moses takes his name from the lawgiver who, according to the biblical narrative, led the Israelites from slavery in Egypt and delivered the Ten Commandments, so his position as a prophet of an animal religion is apt.

Sugarcandy Mountain is an animal version of the medieval English concept of Cockayne, a mythical land of plenty. Cockayne focused on luxury because it was born out of a time when peasants faced arduous physical labour and scant food and when wealth was in the hands of the nobles and the church. It was not heaven but a physical land to which one could travel, if one knew the way. And it was not spiritual:

the bawdy, gluttonous, lazy lifestyle it offered was the opposite of the church's precepts.

Moses' name for this paradise recalls the American song, 'Big Rock Candy Mountain'. First recorded by Harry McClintock in 1928, the song's popularity didn't peak until 1939, towards the end of the Great Depression, when its vision of a hobo version of Cockayne – flowing with food and free of law enforcement – was peculiarly attractive. The Depression itself, when economic difficulties forced people into arduous work and long hours for little pay or food, parallels the animals' experience under Napoleon's rule.

The key difference between Cockayne and Sugarcandy Mountain, however, is that the latter does not occupy the same geographical space as England: Sugarcandy Mountain is heaven. As Moses explains to the animals, it is a place 'to which all animals went when they died' (p.10), as a reward for their struggles during their lifetime.

When Moses first mentions his idea to the animals, 'some of them believed in Sugarcandy Mountain' (p.11). Generally, however, they are uninterested, especially as the Rebellion itself draws on religious imagery to inspire the animals. Animalism is inscribed in the form of the Seven Commandments. 'Beasts of England' speaks of the 'golden future time' when 'Riches more than mind can picture, / Wheat and barley, oats and hay, / Clover, beans and mangel-wurzels / Shall be ours upon that day' (p.7) – such images are remarkably similar to Moses' description of hedges in which sugar and linseed cakes grow.

But when Moses returns later in the novella and repeats his story, 'Many of the animals believed him' (p.78). The erosion of the early principles of the Rebellion leaves room for faith. The promised 'golden future time' has vanished. The commandments on the wall of the barn have been changing almost in front of the animals' eyes. Though the fields of barley have eventuated, 'it was announced that from now onwards all barley would be reserved for the pigs' (p.76), just like the milk and apples before it. As the animals explain it to themselves, 'Their lives now, they reasoned, were hungry and laborious; was it not right and just that a better world should exist somewhere else?' (p.78). Such an attitude would barely have been possible immediately after the Rebellion.

Most significant of all is the changing attitude of the pigs. At first, they take some trouble to convince the other animals that Sugarcandy Mountain is a myth (p.11). By the time Moses returns, however, they make less effort: 'They all declared contemptuously that his stories about Sugarcandy Mountain were all lies, and yet they allowed him to remain on the farm, not working, with an allowance of a gill of beer a day' (pp.78–79).

The myth of Sugarcandy Mountain recalls the famous quotation on the role of religion in socialism from Karl Marx's 1843 text, *Contribution to Critique of Hegel's Philosophy of Right*: 'Religion is the sigh of the oppressed creature, the heart of a heartless world, and the soul of soulless conditions. It is the opium of the people' (often paraphrased as 'religion is the opium of the people' or 'religion is the opium of the masses'.) The pigs encourage Moses because the idea of Sugarcandy Mountain drugs the animals with false hope, stopping them from questioning their laborious and hungry lives and the decay of Animalism. All this costs the pigs only a quarter of a pint of beer a day.

Propaganda

Key quotes

'Now when Squealer described the scene so graphically, it seemed to the animals that they did remember it' (p.54).

'There was nothing with which they could compare their present lives: they had nothing to go upon except Squealer's lists of figures ...' (p.87)

Moses' descriptions of Sugarcandy Mountain are only one of the pigs' propaganda tactics. Propaganda is material specifically designed to influence opinion in favour of or against a particular position, movement or government. Propaganda does serve neutral purposes: for example, for public health campaigns. But the early twentieth century was marked by waves of manipulative, xenophobic propaganda from Europe's totalitarian governments (and beyond), culminating in World War II–era propaganda. The key point is that propaganda is not impartial communication: it promotes a specific viewpoint and seeks a particular audience response. *Animal Farm* showcases three uses of propaganda: propaganda from within Animal Farm the propaganda of neighbouring farmers, and the novella itself as propaganda.

On the farm, propaganda is the province of the pigs, beginning with Major's speech in Chapter I, where he outlines 'a dream of the earth as it will be when Man has vanished' (p.6). Major's speech is propagandist because it promotes a specific response from his audience, inspiring a desire for 'the overthrow of the human race' (p.5). After the Rebellion, the pigs remain the farm's propagandists. For example, Snowball, who has less 'depth of character' than Napoleon, is 'quicker in speech and more inventive' (p.9). He uses this quickness of speech to promote his ambitions for the farm, namely the windmill. Though Snowball seems to be genuinely working for the good of the farm, his eloquent oratory is nevertheless an example of propaganda: he draws the animals an image of a modernised, electrified farm in which the labour is no longer the animals' responsibility, and persuades his listeners of its truth.

Before Snowball's expulsion, Napoleon makes little use of propaganda: for example, when he speaks against the windmill, 'he had spoken for barely thirty seconds, and seemed almost indifferent as to the effect he produced' (p.35). Indeed, the use of propaganda is one of the main disputes between the two leaders: while Snowball argues that they 'must send out more and more pigeons and still up rebellion among the animals on other farms', Napoleon argues for an isolationist, militaristic approach, in which the animals 'procure firearms and train themselves in the use of them' (p.34). But after Snowball's expulsion, propaganda assumes a central role in Napoleon's governance of the farm.

Napoleon's propaganda operates in two directions: outside the farm and inside the farm. Outside the farm, Napoleon maintains the network of pigeons established after the Rebellion, whose sole purpose is to disseminate propaganda: their instructions are 'to mingle with the animals on neighbouring farms, tell them the story of the Rebellion, and teach them the tune of "Beasts of England"' (p.24). He also organises more elaborate acts of propaganda, as when he orders the 'almost empty bins in the store-shed to be filled nearly to the brim with sand, which was then covered up with what remained of the grain and meal' (p.50), deceiving Whymper into believing that the animals are not suffering food shortages.

But Napoleon's most sustained use of propaganda is against the animals themselves. The further he moves away from Animalism, the more elaborate his devotions to the images of the Rebellion become. Take, for example, the 'Spontaneous Demonstrations' that Napoleon insists take place once a week. He orders these late in his rule, after 'Beasts of England' is banned, the pigs have moved into the farmhouse, and the show trials have taken place. The demonstrations are exercises in propaganda because they emphasise the symbols of the Rebellion, to disguise the leadership's change in stance. Though the animals sometimes complain, the propaganda works:

> They found it comforting to be reminded that, after all, they
> were truly their own masters and that the work they did was for
> their own benefit. So that what with the songs, the processions,
> Squealer's lists of figures, the thunder of the gun, the crowing of
> the cockerel and the fluttering of the flag, they were able to forget
> that their bellies were empty, at least part of the time (p.77).

This is Napoleon's most sustained act of propaganda (apart, perhaps, from the re-imagination of Snowball as the farm's enemy): maintaining the animals' belief that they are their own masters.

It can also be argued that *Animal Farm* is itself a form of propaganda, given how negatively it presents totalitarianism. Orwell acknowledged that the novella has a political purpose, and some critics describe it as anti-Soviet propaganda. Like other political texts, it also served a propagandist purpose within Soviet Russia. Before the end of the Cold War (in 1991), *Animal Farm* (along with Orwell's later novel, *Nineteen Eighty-Four*) was a forbidden book in Eastern bloc countries, available only through *samizdat* copies. *Samizdat* (meaning 'self-published', from Russian) was a dissident (rebellious) activity in Eastern bloc nations, involving copying censored books by hand and passing them from reader to reader. In this way, Orwell's book continued to travel clandestinely though the system that it critiqued.

DIFFERENT INTERPRETATIONS

Different interpretations arise from different responses to a text. Over time, a text will give rise to a wide range of responses from its readers, who may come from various social or cultural groups and live in very different places and historical periods. These responses can be published in newspapers, journals and books by critics and reviewers, or they can be expressed in discussions among readers in the media, classrooms, book groups and so on. While there is no single correct reading or interpretation of a text, it is important to understand that an interpretation is more than a personal opinion – it is the justification of a point of view on the text. To present an interpretation of the text based on your point of view you must use a logical argument and support it with relevant evidence from the text.

Critical viewpoints

Literary critics disagree about the extent to which the allegory in *Animal Farm* refers solely to Soviet Russia. This is apparent in American scholarship written during the Cold War (1946–91), when communism was of particular concern in the United States. Such scholarship argues that *Animal Farm* should be read exclusively as a parable about Soviet Russia. For example, John Rodden (a major Orwell scholar) argues:

> Like most allegories, *Animal Farm* operates by framing one-to-one correspondences between the literal and symbolic levels. Its events and characters function as a simple story on the literal level. But they also operate on a symbolic level for readers who know the 'code'. In this case, the key code is the history of Soviet Communism (Rodden, 2003, p.72).

Rodden then links plot points in the novella to events in Soviet Russia and argues that, 'If a reader misses such allegorical correspondences, he or she may completely misread the book' (p.72). John Rossi also gives an excellent overview of this tendency in American scholarship.

In contrast, Robert Pearce argues:

> Everyone is familiar with the parallels between Russian history
> and the plot of *Animal Farm*. Perhaps indeed we are over-familiar
> with them, for the details of the book had a wider totalitarian
> purpose than to any one country, and Orwell borrowed from
> Italian history ('Mussolini is always right') and from German, as
> well as from Russian (Pearce, 1998, p.66).

Certainly, reading *Animal Farm* without any knowledge of the events
of Russian history would lessen the impact of the text. But reading it
as exclusively applying to Soviet Russia will also dim the richness of
Orwell's critique of totalitarianism. It is necessary to be aware of this
concern when reading critiques of *Animal Farm*.

Animal Farm is under-represented in critical literature compared to
some of Orwell's other works. As Morris Dickstein puts it:

> Today Orwell is rightly admired as a superb essayist. There's
> also a vastly greater critical literature on *Nineteen Eighty-Four*
> than on *Animal Farm*, though they pursue the same critique of
> Stalinist totalitarianism by different means. *Nineteen Eighty-Four*
> … is seen as a book for grownups, a serious human drama.
> *Animal Farm*, on the other hand, has been typed as a primer for
> the uninitiated, a beautifully crafted tale only a few cuts above
> propaganda (Dickstein, 2007, p.134).

The 'vastly greater critical literature' on *Nineteen Eighty-Four* can
be seen in Paul Schlueter's 'Trends in Orwell Criticism: 1968–1983',
an excellent bibliography of early essays on Orwell. In the fifteen years
Schlueter covers, he isolates thirty-two works on *Nineteen Eighty-Four*
and ten on *Animal Farm*; one of the latter essays is actually on both texts.

Very little (if any) scholarship of *Animal Farm* analyses the text without
referring to its allegorical meanings. Of the ten articles that Schlueter lists,
for example, the majority have in the title the word 'politics' or 'satire', or
both. Such a focus is understandable. The risk is in *how* this allegorical
content is interpreted. Because *Animal Farm* is such a politically charged

novella, it is often co-opted for political purposes that are at odds with Orwell's own outlook. In Ian Williams' words, 'the popularity of the Orwell "brand" has led many people to misrepresent his views since his death, and to appropriate his prestige for their own political purposes' (Williams, 2007, p.100).

Orwell consistently identified himself as a democratic socialist. The fact that he excluded Soviet Communism from the category of socialism does not make his politics any less left wing: he excluded it because he felt it had no bearing on true socialism, and actually damaged the socialist cause. Therefore, any analysis that argues that Orwell's criticism of Soviet Communism means he was a proponent of either capitalism or strong, hierarchical government must be treated with extreme caution.

Two interpretations

Interpretation 1: It is impossible to understand *Animal Farm's* critique of totalitarianism without also understanding the history of Soviet Russia

Animal Farm was written during a highly specific historical period. The dates November 1943 to February 1944 are inscribed in the body of the text (p.95): they appear before the words 'The End,' making them part of the novella itself. As such, we are encouraged to read the novella in the light of the events of this time. Orwell himself said that *Animal Farm* was written as a means of exposing the abuses of the Soviet system. Readers therefore need to bring some knowledge of the history of Soviet Russia to their understanding of the text.

Knowing the history of Soviet Russia allows us to understand the characters' behaviour, where this might be otherwise unclear. For example, the narrative structure of the novella prevents us from knowing what the pigs are thinking and planning. As such, we need to rely on our understanding of Joseph Stalin's attempts to increase his personal power after Lenin's death to understand Napoleon's increasingly dictatorial stance.

Similarly, reading the events of the novella through the history of Soviet Russia increases our sense of the inevitability of the novella's events. We assume that Napoleon will turn on his followers and reinforce his regime with the brutal suppression of any sedition. We cannot predict precisely when in the course of the novella the show trials and summary executions will occur, but we know that they will. This sense of inevitability, engendered by the novella's connection to Soviet Russia, also enhances the trepidation with which we approach Boxer's death: once he becomes too ill to work, we can anticipate that he, loyal to an early system of government that no longer exists, will be purged. The connection to events in Soviet history ensures that we read the novella differently than we would a purely fictional work; we anticipate certain events, even if we can't predict their specific form.

Finally, understanding the historical background of the novella adds richness to the symbols that Orwell uses. For example, the key symbol in the second half of the book is the windmill, which the animals repeatedly build and which is repeatedly destroyed. As a symbol, the windmill represents the futility of the animals' dreams of a new utopia; instead of moving forward into a world free of Man, in which animals rule themselves, they are simply re-treading the same ground, exchanging one set of masters for another. But the symbol becomes richer if we read it not as a single, repeated act, but as representative of multiple failed economic plans and resultant famines.

Animal Farm does stand as a self-contained work of fiction. But Orwell's allegory is so intricate, detailed and all-encompassing that readers need to bring an understanding of the history of Soviet Russia to their analysis of the text.

Interpretation 2: *Animal Farm* shows the construction and collapse of a self-contained totalitarian system

Animal Farm has traditionally been read as a tightly focused allegory about events between the October Revolution of 1917 and the Tehran Conference in 1943. Certainly, it would be inaccurate to deny that Orwell specifically drew on Russian history (among other inspirations) for his 'fairy story'. But this raises a concern about modern comprehension of the novella. Ninety years after the October Revolution and twenty years after the end of the Cold War, most of us lack the detailed understanding of those events that readers would have had in 1943. Will modern readers be able to understand Orwell's satire now that the regime on which it was largely based has fallen?

Though Soviet Russia was the inspiration for *Animal Farm*, the novella shows the construction and the collapse of a self-contained political system, allowing us to understand Orwell's satire even without the key to the original allegory. We follow the entire progress of revolution, from its inception in old Major's speech, through the Rebellion itself, to counter-revolutionary attacks against the farm and the final collapse of the revolution into decadence and dictatorship. Animalism – Orwell's animal-based rewriting of the principles of communism – is described in as much detail to us as it is to the animals that believe in it. The totalitarian system in *Animal Farm* is self-contained: its genesis, development and collapse are all narrated.

Furthermore, the reader is deeply involved in the Rebellion. Because of the limitations of the narration, we are as ignorant as the other animals: we cannot tell what the pigs are thinking or planning. As a result, we are shocked when the Rebellion takes a violent turn (in the show trials) and when trust is betrayed (in Boxer's death). We react to these shocks whether or not we are able to predict the events (from our knowledge of Soviet Russia). We react because, to us as much as to the other animals, the pigs' behaviour is such a comprehensive betrayal of the principles of Animalism in which we have been immersed.

Although written as an allegory for a specific regime, *Animal Farm* sets out its own context-specific philosophy (Animalism), presents the entire span of the failed revolution, presents characters who sincerely believe in but are betrayed by their leaders, and immerses us in these events. Its critique of totalitarianism is as self-contained as it is allegorical.

Soviet Russia has passed into history, but the broader political practice that we call totalitarianism has not. As long as totalitarianism remains, *Animal Farm* remains relevant as a critique of the abuse of power.

QUESTIONS & ANSWERS

This section focuses on your own analytical writing on the text, and gives you strategies for producing high-quality responses in your coursework and exam essays.

Essay writing – an overview

An essay is a formal and serious piece of writing that presents your point of view on the text, usually in response to a given essay topic. Your 'point of view' in an essay is your interpretation of the meaning of the text's language, structure, characters, situations and events, supported by detailed analysis of textual evidence.

Analyse – don't summarise

In your essays it is important to avoid simply summarising what happens in a text:

- A **summary** is a description or paraphrase (retelling in different words) of the characters and events. For example: 'Macbeth has a horrifying vision of a dagger dripping with blood before he goes to murder King Duncan'.

- An **analysis** is an explanation of the real meaning or significance that lies 'beneath' the text's words (and images, for a film). For example: 'Macbeth's vision of a bloody dagger shows how deeply uneasy he is about the violent act he is contemplating – as well as his sense that supernatural forces are impelling him to act'.

A limited amount of summary is sometimes necessary to let your reader know which part of the text you wish to discuss. However, always keep this to a minimum and follow it immediately with your analysis of what this part of the text is really telling us.

Plan your essay

Carefully plan your essay so that you have a clear idea of what you are going to say. The plan ensures that your ideas flow logically, that your argument remains consistent and that you stay on the topic. An essay plan should be a list of **brief dot points** – no more than half a page. It includes:

- your central argument or main contention – a concise statement (usually in a single sentence) of your overall response to the topic (see 'Analysing a sample topic' for guidelines on how to formulate a main contention)

- three or four dot points for each paragraph indicating the main idea and evidence/examples from the text – note that in your essay you will need to *expand* on these points and *analyse* the evidence.

Structure your essay

An essay is a complete, self-contained piece of writing. It has a clear beginning (the introduction), middle (several body paragraphs) and end (the last paragraph or conclusion). It must also have a central argument that runs throughout, linking each paragraph to form a coherent whole.

See examples of introductions and conclusions in the 'Analysing a sample topic' and 'Sample answer' sections.

The introduction establishes your overall response to the topic. It includes your main contention and outlines the main evidence you will refer to in the course of the essay. Write your introduction *after* you have done a plan and *before* you write the rest of the essay.

The body paragraphs argue your case – they present evidence from the text and explain how this evidence supports your argument. Each body paragraph needs:

- a strong **topic sentence** (usually the first sentence) that states the main point being made in the paragraph

- **evidence** from the text, including some brief quotations

- **analysis** of the textual evidence explaining its significance and explanation of how it supports your argument

- **links back to the topic** in one or more statements, usually towards the end of the paragraph.

Connect the body paragraphs so that your discussion flows smoothly. Use some linking words and phrases like 'similarly' and 'on the other hand', though don't start every paragraph like this. Another strategy is to use a significant word from the last sentence of one paragraph in the first sentence of the next.

Use key terms from the topic – or similes for them – throughout, so the relevance of your discussion to the topic is always clear.

The conclusion ties everything together and finishes the essay. It includes strong statements that emphasise your central argument and provide a clear response to the topic.

Avoid simply restating the points made earlier in the essay – this will end on a very flat note and imply that you have run out of ideas and vocabulary. The conclusion is meant to be a logical extension of what you have written, not just a repetition or summary of it. Writing an effective conclusion can be a challenge. Try using these tips:

- Start by linking back to the final sentence of the second-last paragraph – this helps your writing to 'flow', rather than just leaping back to your main contention straight away.

- Use similes and expressions with equivalent meanings to vary your vocabulary. This allows you to reinforce your line of argument without being repetitive.

- When planning your essay, think of one or two broad statements or observations about the text's wider meaning. These should be related to the topic and your overall argument. Keep them for the conclusion, since they will give you something 'new' to say but still follow logically from your discussion. The introduction will be focused on the topic, but the conclusion can present a wider view of the text.

Essay topics

1 'Now if there was one thing that the animals were completely certain of, it was that they did not want Jones back.' What role does fear play in *Animal Farm*?

2 'Orwell's satire would be impossible if he wrote about people rather than animals.' Discuss.

3 How does Orwell's use of a third-person, limited narrator influence our understanding of *Animal Farm*?

4 'If we don't understand the history of Soviet Russia, we can't understand *Animal Farm*.' To what extent is this statement true?

5 '*Animal Farm* manages to raise its readers' consciousness without really moving them at the deepest level' (Morris Dickstein). To what extent is this statement true?

6 'The pigs could not have become dictators if the other animals had not allowed them to do so.' Discuss.

7 'Napoleon is not entirely without redeeming characteristics.' Discuss.

8 TS Eliot said that the pigs in *Animal Farm* are 'far more intelligent than the other animals, and therefore the best qualified to run the farm … what was needed (someone might argue), was not more communism but more public-spirited pigs'. Discuss.

9 '*Animal Farm* is optimistic about socialism, but cannot show it operating effectively.' Discuss.

10 '*Animal Farm* blurs the lines between history and memory.' Discuss.

Vocabulary for writing on *Animal Farm*

Allegory: A narrative that works both on a primary level as a straightforward story and a secondary level as a representation of real people and events (or, in some cases, abstract ideals, such as love or honour).

Anthropomorphism: The attribution of human qualities to non-human things, usually deities, animals or plants. Orwell limits the animals according to their physical attributes – for example, the way the pigs are tasked with painting or doing the milking, because their cloven hooves are suited for such tasks – but anthropomorphises them in other respects, such as their ability to speak English.

Beast fable: A short narrative that provides an example of human morality or social principles, in which anthropomorphised animals take human roles.

Dystopia: Literally, 'bad place' – from the Greek *dys* (bad) + *topos* (place) – the opposite of a utopia. Dystopias are fictions in which modern trends (such as scientific advances) have led to a violent, repressive future, where characters are subjected to strict government control and stripped of their individuality. Utopias have a long history, but the use of the term dystopia is comparatively recent: one of the earliest examples is Orwell's own *Nineteen Eighty-Four* (1949), still regarded as a benchmark of the genre. *Animal Farm* has dystopian elements, particularly when the animals' existence under Napoleon is compared to their utopian dreams in the novella's beginning.

Fairytale: See **Genre, Structure & Language**

Analysing a sample topic

This section leads you through the analysis of a single question and the planning of a response.

'The pigs could not have become dictators if the other animals had not allowed them to do so.' Discuss.

This question focuses on both the pigs and the other animals. To fully answer the question, you need to analyse the behaviour of both parties. The other key word is 'allowed'. This can be interpreted in two ways: that the animals either *actively* or *passively* encourage the pigs' increasing control. Your essay will be stronger if you decide which one it is (active or passive) and argue accordingly.

Sample introduction

The rebellion on Animal Farm fails because it becomes a totalitarian dictatorship, controlled by a leader more interested in luxury and personal power than in the animals under his authority. However, just as it takes the combined power of the animals to overthrow Jones, it requires their combined collusion to keep the pigs in power. For most, this is merely passive agreement with the pigs' plans; for others, it is an active choice. However, the pigs do not rely entirely on the animals' agreement. Rather, they gradually build a power structure in which disagreement becomes increasingly difficult.

Body paragraph 1

The animals' agreement is necessary to keep the pigs in power.

- Describe how the novella begins with a rebellion against a strong, dictatorial leader. Napoleon could be overthrown by the combined might of the other animals, just as Jones was.

- Show an awareness that the animals grant the pigs a particular degree of authority even before the Rebellion takes place, e.g., 'The work of teaching and organising the others fell naturally upon the pigs, who were generally recognised as being the cleverest of the animals' (p.9).

- Analyse the way in which the pigs play on the 'natural' order of things (i.e., that they are the cleverest and the best suited for leadership) even while overthrowing the 'natural order' (i.e., that Man is dominant over animals).

Body paragraph 2
Most animals on the farm assume only a passive role in maintaining the pigs' power.

- Define what is meant by *passive* involvement: in this case, it is not that the animals actively promote the pigs' power, but that they passively accept the gradual increases in authority.

- The key example here is the pigs' claiming of the milk and apples. Emphasise two main points in your analysis: this happens within hours of the original revolution and the animals, by not arguing at this point, establish that they are willing to accept the pigs' behaviour.

- You can qualify the argument here by pointing out that some of the animals (e.g., Boxer) are not particularly intelligent, and that the pigs consciously exploit the other animals' loyalty to Animalism.

Body paragraph 3
Some of the animals, however, take an active role in allowing the pigs' increasingly dictatorial control of the farm. Two differing types of activity can be discussed in this paragraph.

- Firstly, discuss the other animals who support the pigs. Chief among these are the dogs who serve as Napoleon's secret police. However, you might also consider Moses the raven, who serves a useful purpose for the pigs.

- Secondly, the character of Benjamin the donkey is a useful example here. Because he can see what the pigs are doing but does nothing, he could be considered a passive character. But because Benjamin is more intelligent than the other animals and recognises what the pigs are doing (e.g., when Squealer changes the commandments, p.73), his is an *active* choice to do nothing. Compare his general behaviour, for example, to his attempts to save Boxer.

Body paragraph 4

The animals' passivity is not the only means by which the pigs retain control.

- Having established that the other animals play a key role in the pigs' power, note that this is not the sole way in which the pigs retain control.

- Isolate activities that are outside the control of the other animals, e.g., Napoleon's control of the secret police, the show trials, the brutal crackdown on the chickens' protest at the sale of their eggs.

- This paragraph refines the argument by, firstly, establishing that the pigs don't rely entirely on the passivity of the other animals and, secondly, emphasising the way in which the animals are induced to support the pigs through threats and lies.

Sample conclusion

Animal Farm shows the dangers of permitting a ruthless leader to assume too much power. However, the novella is careful not to solely blame either the leader himself or his subjects. Napoleon certainly enforces his rule rigidly, through threats, intimidation, lies and the summary execution of dissidents. But his position of power could not have been consolidated if the other animals had disputed the small privileges that the pigs claimed early in the revolution. The pigs benefit as much from the passivity of some animals as they do from the active support of others.

SAMPLE ANSWER

"Now if there was one thing that the animals were completely certain of, it was that they did not want Jones back." What role does fear play in Animal Farm?

Fear is the single most powerful influence on the animal revolution in *Animal Farm*. The animals rebel out of fear, but fear becomes the weapon by which their new masters control them. The pigs invent various bogeymen to frighten the other animals: first Jones and then the exiled Snowball. From the bogeymen, Napoleon progresses to his secret police, who instil in the animals a fear of sudden, violent death. By manipulating their fears, Napoleon retains his control of the animals, even though they have already rebelled against one cruel master.

The animals are induced to rebel by hunger as well as fear. The ultimate catalyst is hunger, when the drunken Jones and his idle farm-workers fail to feed the animals one night. But the seeds of the Rebellion have been planted by Major's speech, which focuses as much on fear as it does on hunger. Major points out to the pigs that 'every one of you will scream your lives out at the block within a year' and insists, 'To that horror we all must come'. His vivid descriptions of the various deaths that await the animals are a powerful incitement to action. The animals already know that they will die, but Major's speech plays on their fears. When Major speaks of revolution, he convinces the animals that their coming deaths are not, as they have believed, a part of the natural order of things. After the Rebellion, however, the pigs manipulate the animals' existing fear for their own purposes.

The pigs' first step is to create various bogeymen, which they use to direct the animals' behaviour into certain channels. The first bogeyman is Jones himself. The pigs first use him as a threat as early as the incident of the milk and the apples, when Squealer justifies the pigs claiming these items by saying, 'Do you know what would happen if we pigs failed in our duty? Jones would come back!' This fear is reinforced when Jones does return, to be defeated in the Battle of the Cowshed.

Jones remains an effective bogeyman until he is replaced by a second bogeyman: Snowball.

Snowball is an even more effective bogeyman than Jones, because he is a former comrade. If Snowball can be 'a dangerous character and a bad influence,' then any of their comrades could also turn on them. Snowball is such a frightening figure to the animals that, 'Whenever anything went wrong it became usual to attribute it to Snowball'. To the pigs, this 'usual' behaviour is also useful: Snowball's alleged malevolence becomes a way for them to control the animals and simultaneously avoid blame for anything that goes wrong on the farm. Eventually, the animals come to believe that Snowball has near-supernatural influence, 'as though Snowball were some kind of invisible influence, pervading the air about them'. This fear reinforces Napoleon's influence, as the animals come to rely on him to keep them safe from Snowball. However, Napoleon does not rely entirely on invisible bogeymen to frighten the animals.

As Napoleon's power increases, he employs open intimidation tactics to frighten the other animals. The earliest of these is his secret police, the nine puppies he trained 'in such seclusion that the rest of the farm soon forgot their existence'. The fact that Napoleon began training the puppies almost immediately after the Rebellion suggests that he was always planning to rule by fear. Fear of the dogs reaches its apex at the show trails; as each animal confesses, 'the dogs promptly tore their throats out'. The only one who is not frightened of the dogs is Boxer, but few of the other animals have his overwhelming physical strength. The animals' fear at this point is not the fear of the supernatural that marked their relations with the spectre of Snowball, but a very real fear of sudden, violent death. But Napoleon has brought them to this state of terror in gradual stages, by using fear as a means of controlling their behaviour since the earliest days of the Rebellion.

Napoleon retains his position as undisputed dictator of Animal Farm by manipulating the animals until they are as afraid to confront him as they are to try to operate the farm without him. The earliest uses of fear play on real threats to the animals, particularly the return of their unkind former master. But as Jones ceases to be a threat, after the Battle of the Cowshed, Napoleon and his pigs invent other threats – namely Snowball and the secret police – to keep the animals from overthrowing their new masters the way they overthrew their old one. As such, fear is the most potent weapon at Napoleon's command.

REFERENCES & READING

Text

Orwell, George 1945, *Animal Farm: A Fairy Story*, Penguin, London.

Other references

Dickstein, Morris 2007, '*Animal Farm*: History as Fable', in John Rodden (ed.), *The Cambridge Companion to George Orwell*, Cambridge University Press, Cambridge, pp.133–45.

Orwell, George 1947, 'Preface to *Kolghosp Tvaryn* [*Animal Farm*]', http://orwell.ru/library/novels/Animal_Farm/english/epfc_go

Orwell, George 2004, 'Why I Write', in *Why I Write*, Penguin Books, London, pp.1–10.

Pearce, Robert 1998, 'Orwell, Tolstoy, and *Animal Farm*', *Review of English Studies*, vol. 49, no. 193, pp.64–69.

Rodden, John 2003, 'Appreciating *Animal Farm* in the New Millennium', *Modern Age*, vol. 45, pp.67–6.

Rodden, John (ed.) 2007, *The Cambridge Companion to George Orwell*, Cambridge University Press, Cambridge.

Rossi, John P 1981, 'America's View of George Orwell', *The Review of Politics*, vol. 43, no.4, pp.572–81.

Schlueter, Paul 1984, 'Trends in Orwell Criticism: 1968–1983', *College Literature*, vol. 11, no. 1, pp.94–112.

Williams, Ian 2007, 'Orwell and the British Left', in John Rodden (ed.), *The Cambridge Companion to George Orwell*, Cambridge University Press, Cambridge, pp.100–11.

Zipes, Jack 1991, *Fairy Tales and the Art of Subversion*, Routledge, London.

notes